THE
FREEZER COOKING MANUAL

FROM
30 DAY GOURMET

A MONTH OF MEALS MADE EASY

30 DAY GOURMET
PRESS

The Freezer Cooking Manual from 30 Day Gourmet: A Month of Meals Made Easy may be purchased for educational, business, or sales promotional use. For more information please contact: *Special Markets Department*, 30 Day Gourmet Press 30½ E. Main Street, Brownsburg IN 46112 or call 1-800-962-6825 or fax 1-317-852-1946.

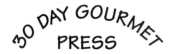

30 ½ E. Main Street
Brownsburg IN 46112
(317)852-8499; (800) 962-6825
Fax: (317) 852-1946
Email: office@30daygourmet.com
Website: www.30daygourmet.com

Photography by Jay Tobias & Michael Phillips
Cover photo kitchen courtesy of Advance Community Christian Church
Editorial Assistance by Barbara North

Library of Congress Catalog Card Number: 99-095247

Wohlenhaus, Tara and Slagle, Nanci
    The Freezer Cooking Manual from 30 Day Gourmet: A Month of Meals Made Easy /
    Tara Wohlenhaus and Nanci Slagle. – Brownsburg, IN: 30 Day Gourmet Press, ©1999.

    ISBN: 0-9664467-1-2
    1. Cookery   2. Title

Printed in the United States of America

We dedicate this book to our mothers

Dorothy Mayes
and
Helen Tillman

one on earth, the other in heaven.

Thank you for demonstrating a thirst for living,
a taste for adventure, and a craving for the
only food that truly satisfies a soul.

Here's what others are saying about
The Freezer Cooking Manual from 30 Day Gourmet:

Cooks, Parents & Families say:

Good for you ladies! As a working mother with four children under 10 years old – you just may be my heroes.
mom of 4 from Pennsylvania

My friend and I are having a great time with this. Our husbands are proud of us and our kids aren't hungry anymore. We're not running through the drive-thru or making a meal out of soccer field food. Thank you for inspiring us! It's well worth it and we're hooked. **busy mom from Missouri**

The best part about 30 Day Gourmet cooking is how much my husband brags about our full freezer to all of our friends. As a working mom, this has been a godsend. My kids love the recipes.
teacher from Iowa

Although we are a small family, I was glad to see that is not a problem because your system isn't just geared to "large" families. This is a true FAMILY cookbook. Thank you for easy to follow instructions and ingredients I can pronounce.
dual career family from New York

Just awesome! I'm a whole new person come 6 pm.
home school mom from Florida

After researching all the "once-a-month" cooking books out there, yours is BY FAR the most complete, organized and thorough program we have found. **cooking couple from Indiana**

My 18 year old son and I made several meals for him to put in single serving sizes and take to his college apartment. He finds this to be a quick and easy way to have home-cooked meals.
working mom from Ohio

Penny Pinchers say:

This cookbook is the best money I have ever invested! **frugal family from Washington**

I recently compared my budget from a "before 30 Day Gourmet" year to an "after 30 Day Gourmet" year. What a surprise! I had cut our grocery spending by almost $1000!!! Thanks for the wonderful book!
computer analyst from California

Great book! It's the only way I cook anymore! I just love the recipes. No one can believe they have been pulled out of the freezer and I am saving LOTS of money! **day care provider from Virginia**

Seniors say:

Your method works well for retirees who do not want to spend every day thinking of what to cook when we have more fun things to do. The 6 person meal gives us 3 meals in the freezer. I have enjoyed your recipes so much and tell everyone who will listen about this method of cooking!
retired secretary from Texas

I just started my daughter-in-law in freezer cooking and she loves it! I had been cooking this way for years but your cooking manual made it easier to teach her how to do it.
active grandma from Michigan

My kids are all grown and gone. This is a great way to cook for the two of us. We travel frequently and it works well to bring made-ahead items along in our motor home freezer.
rv'ers from Minnesota (mostly)

TABLE OF CONTENTS

Dear Friend in the kitchen,

Congratulations on your decision to try (at least once more!!) to organize your cooking. Only those of us who have sung the, *It's 5 p.m. and time to fix dinner - whatever it is I doubt it's a winner,* blues know the stress created by this one little "task". We know how you feel. Both of us remember supper schedules that read like this:

Sunday:	help yourself leftovers
Monday:	taco drive-thru
Tuesday:	tuna sandwiches & chips
Wednesday:	ground beef "helper"
Thursday:	eggs and sausage links
Friday:	pizza pizza
Saturday:	hot dogs/macaroni & cheese

If your meals are similar to these you're not alone! Researchers now tells us that "most" families in America only eat one "home-cooked" meal a week. Why change now? Because deep down, beyond the busy schedules and ever-present fatigue, most of us have similar desires for our evening meal:
1. We want to be together with people we love.
2. We want our food to be nutritious and well-liked.
3. We want to spend our money wisely.

Tara and Nanci

The FREEZER COOKING MANUAL from 30 Day Gourmet could change your life!

Next week your dinner menus could be filled with home cooked foods that you actually look forward to eating! Wonderful main dishes, salads, vegetables and side dishes, and desserts can come from your freezer. These prepared and frozen foods are so delicious and convenient that you will not want to go back to your old methods of meal planning.

We met at church back in 1990 and soon struck up a friendship, sharing with each other the different triumphs and stresses in our lives. Even though one of us loves to cook and one of us hates to cook, we discovered that we each were struggling to get decent meals on the table. Seven small children and outside interests had made meal preparations a real chore. Nanci became what she calls a "crisis cook" - not thinking about dinner until the last possible moment. Tara was trying to make wonderful meals "like Momma used to make", but was never getting it done. We agreed that something HAD to change.

Feeding our families a great meal every day of the month was our first goal, hence the name "30 DAY GOURMET". We began to cook together and make 30 entrees in one day, every month. This was so successful for us that we began to add to the number of frozen entrees we made and also included some frozen fruit salads, vegetables and side dishes. We now assemble about three months' worth of dinner entrees in a single, very long day using our plan. But don't think that you have to do things *our* way.

Our goal in writing this manual is to aid you in preparing quantities of foods for the freezer. For most people, the main dish seems to be the problem. If we can gain control of this part, then we can usually come up with side dishes, fruits and vegetables to round out the meal.

We hope that people using this book will consider making 24 to 30 entrees in a single cooking spree. Families with children, seniors, and singles all could benefit from having good food at their fingertips. For some, cooking on the weekend and preparing one month or one week's worth of foods will suit your needs. Other people will use our plan only occasionally and make enough to get through the "busy season", or vacation meals to transport in coolers to the cabin or condo. Still others will use this manual to help prepare food for a family member with special dietary needs. This book could be the answer to all your cooking dilemmas!

Cooking the 30 DAY GOURMET way is worth whatever it takes to make it work for you. Since the summer of 1993 when we began cooking together, we have learned a ton. We have made all the mistakes (2 gallons of burned white sauce, missed ingredients, recipes that didn't get doubled correctly) and dealt with most of the usual and unusual interruptions (husbands "popping in" for lunch, 1-7 kids underfoot, broken answering machines, crying babies, door-to-door salesmen, and even emergency trips to the hospital).

This manual will help you avoid many of these problems. But, of course, even if you do make mistakes and deal with interruptions, remember - it's still worth it!! Nothing beats the relief and great sense of accomplishment we feel when we can take an entree out of the freezer, go to the zoo or our office for the day, and come home to a 10 minute preparation time for dinner. Now even on the crazy days we still enjoy a great homemade meal.

This is a hands-on manual. Make several copies of the worksheet pages as you'll use these each month. Having everything in one place is SO helpful. You may wish to place the worksheet copies and any family favorite recipes you have or begin to accumulate in a three ring binder. We have wasted so much valuable time looking for recipes, searching for last month's ingredient list, and rewriting the same worksheets each time. We are glad to have this organization tool for ourselves, too!

Have fun! And please don't think of 30 DAY GOURMET as another one of those great ideas thought up by superhuman, nearly perfect women. We are just a couple of average women with lots to do and little time to do it in. Our kids' baby books are only half-filled. At this point, we will have to start making things up. We have BOXES of photos waiting for albums. Our closets are still messy, and we don't always check to see if the children's clothes match as they head out the door. Only one of us is a great cook by nature. As our pastor frequently says, "We are all fellow strugglers". This is just one little corner of our lives that we have finally organized and boy does it feel great! So, give **The Freezer Cooking Manual from 30 Day Gourmet** a try and see what happens. We're guessing that it will make your meals more convenient, tastier, less expensive, lots more relaxing, and even enjoyable! Happy (infrequent) cooking - and please let us know how it goes.

Feel free to contact us on our web site at **www.30daygourmet.com**, or through our toll-free telephone number at **1-800-9-MANUAL**. We do not want to sell you a product without offering further customer support. We want you to be as successful as possible! If you have cooking questions, a story to share, or a recipe to contribute, we would love to hear from you!

With our warm (fresh out-of-the-oven) wishes,

Tara Wohlenhaus   **Nanci Slagle**

The Rewards of Freezer Cooking

In our years of experience cooking this way, we have fallen in love with it. We have enjoyed so many benefits from our system. Here are a few that we are sure you will appreciate:

We love the convenience.
> We have a home cooked meal ready whenever one is needed! The **30 DAY GOURMET** plan makes the whole project so much easier. Just choose something from the freezer in the morning or the night before, then don't give it another thought until late afternoon or early evening. It's great!

We love to save $$$$$.
> We know that eating out or going to the market today for tonight's dinner can be very costly. A family of 4 can easily spend $20+ on a fast food dinner or pre-packaged frozen dinners. Using the **Freezer Cooking Manual** lowers our food bills! We spend no more than $3.50-$5.00 for each main dish recipe for our families of 5 and 6. Think of what you could save! And when we do eat out, the kids are thrilled and appreciative because it's a treat!

We have enough to share with others.
> Charity and hospitality seem to be lost arts today. By assembling our food in advance, it's easy to take dinner to the neighbor who is ill, a friend who just had a baby, or the family that recently moved in across the street. By cooking multiples of the same recipe, it's also easy to take another entree out of the freezer for company or to accommodate unexpected guests.

Our health has improved.
> If you are currently dining like the majority of Americans, when you begin to use the **Freezer Cooking Manual** you will naturally eat fewer processed foods, fats, salt, and preservatives because you are in control of the ingredients in each recipe. Like us, you can even boost your fiber, vitamin and mineral intake by planning ahead and freezing your foods! Even meatless main dishes can be a snap using our methods.

We love fresh, home-cooked taste.
> We eat few "pre-packaged" and even fewer "drive-thru" foods. We don't miss them. Will you? We have found that proper packaging methods are the key to fresh flavors. Read on for more information!

We enjoy a greater variety of foods.
> Even good cooks run out of time, energy, and creativity at the end of a long day. In the past, we found ourselves making the same easy, but boring, two or three things each week. Not anymore! We can plan our meals to be as exotic or ordinary as we please. We now enjoy opening the freezer door and making choices between food from several national origins.

We can enjoy more free time.
> By planning our meals in advance, we can enjoy the after school hours and after dinner hours with our children, spouse, or friends. Clean up is drastically reduced. We have fewer pots and pans and large cookware to contend with on a daily basis. We also spend less time in the supermarket!

We prepare our own fast foods.
> Sandwich fillings, hamburger patties, spaghetti sauce, chicken nuggets, etc. . . are great for those especially hectic times when you need dinner QUICK! There are still times when our original dinner time plans get scrapped because of sudden changes in schedules. We can still pull together a meal from the freezer in no time at all.

Frequently Asked Questions

My Schedule is too busy now. How can I take a whole day just to cook?
After you try the **The Freezer Cooking Manual** plan, you will realize that the time you save in meal preparation and cleanup each evening is well worth the time it takes to shop and cook in large quantities.

Do I need to buy a freezer?
Actually, about 30 main dish recipes that will serve 4-6 adults each WILL fit into a standard refrigerator's freezer (see photo on page 33). But it does help to have some extra space. We would suggest asking around, shopping the garage sales and auctions, or sharing space with a neighbor. A full freezer works much more efficiently than a half empty one.

Do I have to be a good cook to do this?
Absolutely not! Only the most basic cooking knowledge is needed for most of these recipes. We attempt to give you very detailed instructions so that even the least experienced cooks can be successful. Maybe you can cook with a partner who has more kitchen experience. (Hint: that's what Nanci does!) In the *Appendix*, we have also included a list of cooking terms and definitions.

How do I come up with the money to get started?
Of course, you realize that you WILL be spending the money on food eventually. Try stocking up on grocery items as you see great sales. After a month or two, you should have most of the ingredients. Have a garage sale, use your Christmas bonus, or earmark that tax return check for some quick cash. Or try just cooking for 2 weeks the first time.

Do I have to spend a lot of money on freezer containers and pans?
Use of freezer bags makes it economical to get started. The foods in them can be thawed and put into your favorite dish for baking. Slowly acquire freezer containers, glass casseroles, and metal baking pans at garage sales and discount stores if you like. Nanci uses freezer bags almost exclusively, while Tara opts for a menagerie.

What if I hate to cook?
But you have to eat, right? So do it ONCE in a great while and get it over with. Or try cooking with a partner and make a party out of it!

Will my freezer foods taste fresh?
Having foods in the freezer just gives you the flexibility to decide WHEN you want to cook or bake "from scratch". We seem to have more energy now for creative side dishes, desserts, and more extravagant company meals. Our recipes are made "from scratch". You can choose to pre-bake your entrees and side dishes so that you only have a short heating up period before meals or just pre-assemble your foods and freeze them to cook after thawing. All the aromas and flavors of fresh cooking remain.

Do I need to be an organized and disciplined person to do this?
We're not organized people, but having a cooking partner really helps keep us accountable. And once you have cooked this way a few times, you won't want to go back to the "old ways". If you choose to cook alone, you just have to set the date, make your plans, and stick to them NO MATTER WHAT!

How do I know what foods freeze successfully?
Keep reading and we'll tell you! Actually, more things do freeze well than don't.

What if I LIKE cooking every night?
That's great! Open a restaurant and we'll come for a visit.

7 Steps to the Freezer Cooking Plan

STEP 1:
SET DATES FOR PLANNING, SHOPPING AND COOKING

STEP 2:
TAKE INVENTORY

STEP 3:
HAVE YOUR PLANNING SESSION

STEP 4:
GO SHOPPING

STEP 5:
PREPARE FOR ASSEMBLY DAY

STEP 6:
ASSEMBLE YOUR ENTREES &
          STOCK THE FREEZER

STEP 7:
CLEAN UP & EVALUATE

Before you begin:
DECIDE IF YOU WILL COOK ALONE OR WITH A FRIEND

Advantages of cooking with a friend.

1. **Share recipes.**
   This really helps with the rut that all cooks fall into-fixing the same things each week. Wouldn't you rather try something you know another family actually eats than a new recipe with 25 ingredients?? Of course, when we had our first planning session together, Tara showed up with her special family recipes that had been passed down to her. Nanci showed up with a recipe cut from the back of a macaroni and cheese box and a list of her favorite dishes from the church potluck.

2. **Share the work.**
   In the long run, it is really much less time-consuming to cook for two families at once. After all, you are getting out all the same appliances, cookware, and ingredients anyway. We have heard of groups of 10 and 12 that get together for a big cooking party. Each person makes enough of one recipe for the whole group. Sometimes the cooks aren't even in the same kitchen. All of the recipes can be assembled at different locations, pooled together in one location and split up evenly between participants. We split up the big tasks between us. Tara does the planning, Nanci does the shopping.

3. **Share the fun!**
   Okay, we admit it. This is what keeps us coming back. We love the 8 hour chat we have in the cooking process. We talk and laugh all day long. At the end of the day, we have had a great time, *and we get to go home with a freezer full of food!* It is amazing how hilarious everything is (even spilled cooking oil) about halfway through the day. We try to do special things for each other to make the day especially nice! Tara makes chicken salad for Nanci and Nanci brings Tara extra large muffins from the local bakery. Another bonus is that we are willing to listen to the "long version" of any story. Cooking with a buddy is a great way to get things "all talked out".

4. **Share the thrill!**
   Although our families are very supportive of our cooking and really enjoy the finished product, they just don't get quite as excited as we do about our cooking accomplishments. When we pull six beautiful quiche from the oven and spread them out on the counter to cool, we have a "moment of silence" to admire our work. We "ooh" and "ahh" over each completed creation!

5. **Share the knowledge and abilities.**
   In our situation, Tara has a broad range of cooking and nutrition knowledge. Nanci contributes math skills and shopping finesse. When we pool our talents and smarts, we really do pretty well and are a lot less afraid to cook together than we would be alone. We all have different gifts and abilities - why not share the wealth?

6. **Share the cookware.**
   One very economical reason for cooking with a partner is that each cook doesn't have to purchase every necessary item. Between the two (or more) of you, you will probably come up with plenty of pans, measuring cups, etc. Only one of you needs a food processor or blender, and a mixer. Tara practically *collects* utensils and appliances. Nanci only owned an electric can opener when we began cooking together.

7. **Share the blame.**
   Something is bound to come up on your planned Assembly Day that will threaten to keep you from the task at hand. A child's ballgame, a cancelled and rescheduled appointment, a call from the boss - all of these things will seem to be valid reasons to put off your Assembly Day. If you have promised a friend that you would spend this day in the kitchen, you are less likely to give in to outside demands. We have each had to say things like, "I'm sorry, but this is the only day *SHE* can cook". The blame game also works if you have botched a recipe. We still occasionally scorch a sauce or do something equally silly. You can always blame the strange food on your cooking partner!

Before you begin:
DECIDE IF YOU WILL COOK ALONE OR WITH A FRIEND

Things to consider when choosing a cooking partner:

✓ *Sizes of your families.*
It helps if you have similar sized families so that you can split everything down the middle. Otherwise, the smaller family will always have lots more meals - which may work out okay too, depending on your lifestyles and eating patterns. Whichever one of us runs out of food first usually buys frozen foods from the other so that we still want to cook at the same time. Just hope that you like what she's selling!!

✓ *Your basic tastes.*
If you each choose your 10 favorite meals and none of them is the same, you probably shouldn't cook together. Most cooks can usually agree on 8-10 recipes! We also make allowances all the time for who likes onions, spices, whole wheat pastas, etc. For example, if we make spaghetti sauce, we make the seasonings in the whole batch suitable to the milder tastes of the Slagle family. After Nanci bags her half, additional spices are added to suit the tastes of the Wohlenhaus family. If you have a family favorite that you can't live without, but your cooking partner is not interested in, make and freeze that recipe on your own time. You could even freeze different components of that recipe on your joint Assembly Day so it is easily put together and cooked on the day you want to eat it.

✓ *Your compatibility.*
Don't just ask the best cook you know to be your **30 DAY GOURMET** cooking partner. A good question to ask yourself is, *"Who would I look forward to spending a whole day with?"* We have run into many mother-daughter, and sister-sister teams. We even know spouses who cook together! Yikes - it wouldn't work for us. We are both categorical " messies", while our husbands are "neat freaks". All we see is the creative energy and accomplishment. Our spouses would only see the enormous mess we were making!

Really, we can see that "messies" and "neat freaks" could work well together as long as they have an understanding. The "messy" would spend all day cooking and making the mess. The "neat freak" would date and label all the packages, arrange the freezer, and meticulously clean up each spill.

We can see where two "neat freaks" cooking together might work too - just expect Assembly Day to last at least two days! The "neat freaks" keep putting things away in the cabinets and then have to get them out over and over again!

Splitting Costs

There are a couple of different ways to split the costs fairly between cooking partners.

1. *Taking home the exact same recipes and amounts of food* –
   Save all receipts and cut the cost down the middle.

2. *Taking home the same recipes, but in different amounts* –
   Split receipts by percentages. I take home 33% of the food, I pay 33% of the total costs. I take home 25 % of the food, I pay 25 % of the total costs.

3. *Taking home a couple of different recipes than your partner(s) and in varying amounts* -
   Figure out per recipe and per serving amounts. Each partner pays for exactly the amount of servings that are being kept.

4. *What Tara and Nanci do:*
   Initially split the food costs down the middle. When one partner runs out of freezer entrees, they are purchased at the average amount each entree costs. For example, if you and your partner make 50 dinner entrees, divide the total amount of money spent by the number of entrees. If you agree that each entree costs $3.75, when one partner runs out of food, the other partner sells the entrees to her cooking pal at the going price.

STEP 1
SET DATES FOR PLANNING, SHOPPING, AND COOKING

Whether you are cooking solo or with a friend, you need a little time to plan. Sometimes we meet at Tara's farm, turn the kids loose and make a day of it, but it doesn't have to take more than a couple hours.

The first time you plan, it will seem to take forever. Going through recipes, thinking of what your family likes, and discussing it all is very time consuming. But you WILL get much quicker!

By all means, *do not try to plan over the phone*. Meet at the park, turn a video on for the kids, or even hire a sitter, but PLAN to spend some time. Set an exact date, time and place. Put it on your calendar and don't let anything keep you from it! At this time, you also need to set your dates for shopping and cooking too. Consult your calendar and leave yourself plenty of time to get the work done. We have heard from a few cooks who tried to plan, shop, and cook in a 24 hour time period. Not a good idea.

Sunday	Monday	Tuesday	Wednesday	Thursday	Friday	Saturday
						Call your cooking partner and set dates to plan, shop and cook.
	Planning day- Review new store ads. Decide what to cook, fill out Tally Sheet and Shopping List.		Shop for groceries and begin Prep Work.	Continue Prep Work, and set up kitchen. Set out equipment needed.	Assembly Day! Assemble food, package, and stock the freezer.	Recuperate!

STEP 2
TAKE INVENTORY

Fill out the On-Hand Inventory List *(Worksheet A)*

Update this list each month before your planning day and bring it with you if you are cooking with a friend.

We keep certain items in stock just for our Assembly Day. We stock rice, tomato paste, pasta, cheeses (frozen), freezer bags, canned tomatoes, frozen diced onions, cooking oil, spices, flour, salt, oatmeal, and many other items that are used consistently for Assembly Day. Lots of these are ordered from our food buying club (see page 139 for more information) or bought ahead on super sales and stored at the house where we usually cook. We split the cost on all of these items.

When taking inventory, actually *look* inside your spice cans and canisters to determine how much you have. We have made the mistake of assuming that there was plenty and ended up short on Assembly Day!

We also write down those items that we each might have around that we are willing to contribute to Assembly Day. Remember, you will save money and space, if you use up what you have first, rather than re-buying things you already have. We "guesstimate" the value of these items so that we each pay our fair share. One *Worksheet A* for each cook's inventory is best, but after each cook has filled one out it helps to start a new list for the combined totals of each ingredient.

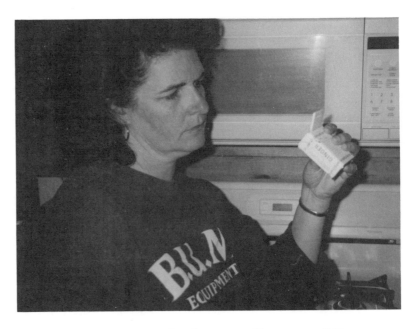

Hmmm . . . is there really enough?
Look inside containers to be sure.

It may seem trivial to the uninitiated to have to actually write down where the different inventory items are stored, but if pantry space is limited in your home, you may actually have a case of tomatoes in your linen closet. We lost a case of mushrooms once, only to stumble upon it months later with the expiration dates long past. Lost and wasted food are no money savings!

Make sure to take inventory of non-food items that you will need too. Freezer bags, trash bags, dish soap, rubber gloves, and disinfectants are all things you may find that you need to purchase for Assembly Day.

Worksheet A Sample

ITEM NAME	QUANTITY	STORAGE PLACE	VALUE
Quick brown rice	3 lbs.	Pantry	$1.40
Whole peeled tomatoes	3/12 oz. cans	Panty	$2.40
Elbow macaroni	8 lbs.	Pantry	$5.40
Shredded cheddar cheese	5 lbs.	Freezer	$12.00
Canned sliced mushrooms	4/10 oz. cans	Pantry	$6.30
Milk	2 gallons	Refrigerator	$4.50
Eggs	2 dozen	Refrigerator	$1.80
Mayonnaise	32 oz.	Pantry	$2.25
Lasagna noodles	2 lbs.	Pantry	$3.50

A Few Inventory Food Storage Tips:

✓ To keep your refrigerated items fresh, keep your refrigerator's temperature set at 35 to 40°F.
✓ To keep refrigerated items that you want to save for Assembly Day as fresh as possible for as long as possible, remember that the back of the top shelf is the coldest. Store the most perishable items there, such as milk, cottage cheese, and other dairy products.
✓ Again, it helps to keep all of these at the designated "cooking house".
✓ If you are stockpiling foods from one month to the next, or you have items you will store for quite a while before using up, try to store them in the coldest cabinet. In other words, store long term items away from your furnace, furnace ducts, oven, clothes dryer and refrigerator exhaust. Heat will shorten the storage life of many items. It is best to keep shelf-stable products in a cool, dry, clean space that stays below 85°F.
✓ Consider using a permanent marker to date your packages so that you can use up the oldest ones first!
✓ Place the newly purchased items on the shelf *behind* the older ones so you are sure to use them up first.
✓ Sunlight will also lessen the quality of long term storage items. We store many of our items in containers that light cannot penetrate. Even a black trash bag will keep out the light!
✓ Store any opened foods in air tight packaging. Food storage containers with a tight seal and food storage bags with a zip-up type seal are helpful with this task.
✓ Be aware of expiration dates. We sometimes plan our recipes so that we use up an item that is nearing that date.
✓ Dry goods like flour, rice, pasta and cornmeal can be stored in the freezer.
✓ If bugs are a problem in your area put your dry goods in the freezer for a few days to kill any possible pests. Then store them in an airtight storage container.
✓ If your items are not stored in a closed pantry, cover the tops of boxes and bags with a cover to keep them from becoming dusty. We have used old sheets and tablecloths.
✓ If your cans are dusty from storage remember to wash them off before you open them up.
✓ If you detect any pests or mold, it is best just to discard the product.
✓ High acid canned goods, such as tomatoes, grapefruit, cherries and pineapple will store for 12 to 18 months.
✓ Low acid canned foods, like stew, carrots and spinach will keep from 2 to 5 years without losing any quality.
✓ If you are using any home-canned goods, play it safe and boil the contents of the jars for at least 10 minutes. Add one minute of boiling time for each 1,000 feet above sea level.
✓ If your canned goods are leaking, bulging, badly dented or rusted, discard the food!
✓ If glass jars containing food are cracked, or have loose or bulging seals, throw them out!
✓ If any can or jar spurts food at you when you open it, throw it out.
✓ Foods with a foul odor or off colors should be discarded!
✓ *NEVER* taste any suspicious foods!
✓ You should report any suspect commercially packaged foods to your local health department. They will want to know where the food was purchased, the date of purchase, the wrapper, can or other packaging.

Write down what you already have on hand so that you don't re-buy those items!

STEP 3
HAVE YOUR PLANNING SESSION

CHOOSE YOUR RECIPES
Choose a list of just 8-10 recipes.
In the beginning, have each cook choose her favorite recipes from this manual as well as any other family favorites you wish to incorporate into your Assembly Day. Almost anything you like to eat can be at least partially made ahead and frozen. If you assemble 3 meals of each recipe, you'll have 24-30 entrees. We have found that between leftovers, occasional dinners out, and entertaining, it's plenty of food for 4-5 weeks. A general rule of thumb is: The more recipes you use, the longer your Assembly Day will be.

Start with tried and true recipes.
Kids (and spouses) may resist unfamiliar food night after night, especially if they are used to eating out or having TV dinners. Don't try more than one new recipe from a book or magazine! Of course, they all look good after a food artist has primped and fluffed them. It really is best to test a new recipe on your own family once before freezing a quantity of it and being committed to eating it 3 times in the next month! You won't be saving any time or money if no one wants to eat the bizarre new entree you serve them. Hamburger patties, sloppy joes, chili, spaghetti sauce, baked chicken, meatloaf, chicken nuggets, and chicken patties are some great beginner ideas.

Always do at least one crock pot meal.
It cooks by itself overnight or during cooking day and all you do is "bag and admire" it. Sometimes we do one crock pot meal the night before and then start another one on Assembly Day morning! Meat sauces, roasts, sandwich fillings, soups and stews and chili are all good candidates for crock pot cooking! When using a crock pot, use small uniform pieces of food, and don't fill it more than 2/3 full.

Pork roast for barbecue sandwich filling – an easy meal that cooks itself.

Consider the season.
In the summer, we prepare lots of hamburger patties, ribs, and meats in marinade for the grill. Chili, soup, and stews are winter favorites.

Plan for entertaining and sharing.
Plan to freeze extra quantities of the recipes you will be sharing with others.

Plan to freeze some commonly used ingredients.
We like to freeze cooked ground meats and poultry in 2 to 3 cup portions by themselves. These are great for impromptu cooking creativity. We also like to have family-sized portions of cooked rice, beans, and pasta bagged and frozen.

Choose a few very versatile recipes.
For some people, the thought of eating the same 8 recipes all month sounds very boring. We recommend you choose a few recipes that begin as one simple idea but can turn into several different meals. For example, if you freeze boneless, skinless chicken breast in *Debbie's Marinade*, you can do several different things with it after thawing. Besides grilling, you could broil it, coat it with crumbs and bake it, or cut it into strips or chunks with a sharp knife and stir-fry it. You could roll the stir-fried strips in a tortilla and call it a fajita, or use them in a sandwich or salad. Other versatile recipes in this book are *Master Meat Mix*, *Taco Rice*, *Master Beef Cube Mix*, and *Chicken* or *Turkey Patties*.

Be aware that some seasonings change in intensity and flavor.
Salt loses some of its flavor in freezing, and may cause an off flavor in high fat items. You can salt after thawing if you wish. Celery and green pepper also lose a little flavor. Black pepper, cloves, bay leaves, onions, and sage become stronger in flavor. Artificial vanilla and curry powder can be very unpleasant! Be assured that the seasonings in our recipes are already adjusted for freezing.

STEP 3

Be sure that your recipe can be frozen.

Food in your freezer, as long as it is at 0° F. or below, does not spoil or become harmful to you. In the big scheme of things, more foods do freeze well than do not. All of the recipes in this manual will freeze fine. When incorporating your own recipes into the system, be sure to use the following guidelines:

Nanci has simmered the turkey breast she bought on sale and froze. It will go into tetrazzini and turkey and noodles.

✓ Don't thaw frozen raw meat and re-freeze it without cooking it thoroughly first. For example, let's imagine that you have hamburger or turkey in your freezer that you purchased while it was on sale. To use this meat in your frozen meals, it needs to be thawed, then cooked before it can be frozen again. Use frozen ground meats for sloppy joe sandwich filling, barbecued beef sandwiches, spaghetti sauce, chili or soup. It can also be made into meatballs that are to be cooked before freezing. If you want to make meatloaf out of this thawed beef, you will have to bake the meatloaf before freezing it. Frozen poultry can be thawed, simmered or baked, then used for turkey and noodles, soups, sandwich fillings, casseroles or enchiladas.

✓ Large pieces of frozen hardboiled egg may have an unpleasant texture after thawing.

✓ Cornstarch thickened sauces, cheese sauces, and gravies made with milk tend to separate when being reheated after freezing. These sauces are acceptable for freezing when they are mixed with other ingredients as in a casserole.

✓ Don't freeze raw vegetables unless they have been blanched. This includes potatoes. Blanching is a short period of cooking that seals in color, texture, vitamins and flavor. Purchased frozen vegetables may be used as they come from the store. They have already been blanched. The exceptions to this rule are diced onions, green pepper and celery. See the blanching information on page 131 for more complete information on blanching specifics. We actually *prefer* buying frozen diced onions to putting three or four pounds of them through the food processor! Frozen diced onions can be found in the freezer case with the rest of the frozen vegetables.

✓ Cured meats, like ham or bacon, should be consumed within one month of freezing because of flavor changes that can occur after that.

✓ Deep fried foods will not stay crispy after thawing and re-heating, and much of the coating may fall off.

✓ Egg and milk replacers freeze well in most recipes.

✓ Fully cooked pasta, dry beans, and rice tend to turn mushy when frozen in liquids. We suggest cooking these starches less than the full recommended time on the packaging directions if they are meant to be frozen in a thin sauce or broth. For example, we undercook long grain brown rice by about 15 minutes. When using quick-cooking brown rice, we shorten the cooking time by 5 minutes. We cook pastas about half the recommended amount of time. For dry beans, we shorten the cooking time by 15 to 20 minutes. You should be able to squash a cooked bean between your fingers with a little pressure. If you cook the beans until the skins split, you have cooked them way too long. Instant white rice may turn to paste if you fully cook it and freeze it in a broth or sauce!

✓ Salad vegetables, like lettuce, cucumbers, tomatoes, and radishes, will not freeze well. Actually, they freeze fine. It's the thawing into a soggy puddle that causes the problem!

✓ Stuffed poultry should not be frozen. It can pose a real health hazard.

STEP 3

Convert your own recipes *(Worksheet B)*

All of the recipes included in this manual have been formatted already to account for assembling 1-6 entrees. When using your own recipes, however, you will need to copy them onto *Worksheet B*. If an 8-10 serving recipe will give you too many leftovers, cut the recipe in half to serve 4-5. If you are single, divide even more, or plan to package in single serving containers.

Look at our *Worksheet B* sample on page 23. This tool will surely save you some headaches on Assembly Day! By multiplying out the ingredients ahead, you save time on Assembly Day and cut down on math errors. Use our Equivalency Charts on pages 126-128 to help you. Make sure and note any changes you will make from the original recipe on the Assembly Directions section of the worksheet. The primary aim of converting the directions is to determine exactly what can be done to this recipe now, so that you will have as little as possible to do on the day you want to eat this food.

Plan your containers

Be sure to mark on your converted recipes what kind of container you will need for freezing each entree. As a general rule, *shallow* containers or ones that allow for *thin layers* are the best. They allow for quick freezing and thawing and usually make good use of limited spaces. Also, consider the size of the container. Don't use one that causes you to have too much air space at the top. That wastes freezer space and allows too much air in with the food. Here are the most common container choices available:

Rigid plastic freezer containers

These are very commonly found in supermarkets, discount stores, or can be purchased at home parties. We have found rigid containers to be a good choice if you have a large freezer where they can be stacked very neatly and are easy to organize. Plastic containers can be re-used until they crack or the seal no longer fits tightly. Containers manufactured specifically for freezing can be expensive, but last much longer. We have tried the "so cheap you can afford to throw them away" containers made by the same companies who make good quality freezer bags. They appear to do a fine job for the most part. Just make sure the seals fit properly. The most convenient rigid freezer containers are those that can go from freezer to microwave to table to refrigerator. We do *NOT* recommend re-using margarine and similar tubs! They are quite inferior containers for freezing. We have found that rectangular freezer containers make better use of valuable freezer space than round ones.

Leave air space at the top of rigid containers to allow for expansion of the food.

Do not pour very hot or boiling foods into plastic containers. Cool the foods first, and allow adequate space at the top of the container to allow liquids to expand while freezing. About 1/2 inch of air at the top of a quart of liquids is plenty.

Freezer labels should be applied to your containers, marked with the date, contents, and any cooking instructions you wish to include. Some people use masking tape, but it will sometimes peel off the container in the freezer. Freezer labels can usually be found near the freezer containers and freezer wraps in larger supermarkets.

Freezer bags

These can be a good choice for homes with limited freezer space area specifically because they pack into such space efficient shapes. Nanci uses freezer bags almost exclusively. Make sure you purchase bags manufactured for freezing. Use a permanent marker to label the bags with the contents and date *before putting food in the bag*. We even recommend writing a simplified version of cooking directions on the bags. This is so that we don't have to drag out a cookbook to make dinner. This also enables others to begin a meal for you when you need an extra hand. Cooled food is placed in the bag, all possible air is removed, and the bag is sealed. You should flatten the bags so they will lie flat and thin in your freezer. We remove the excess air in a couple of ways. Each method is used for different kinds of recipes.

The Squeegee Method:
Seal the bag from one corner to the other, leaving just a small opening at one end. Use the palm of your hand to work the air from the bottom of the bag to the top. Flatten the bag as you go. When all possible air is worked out of the bag, finish sealing it. This method works best for soft, formless foods like stew, chicken and noodles, and meatloaf mixture.

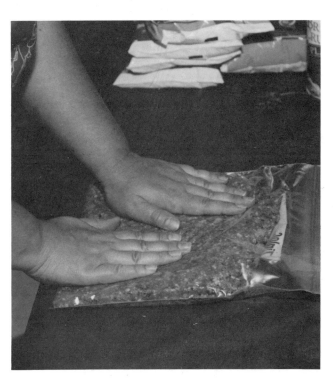

The Straw Method:
Place cooled food, or a pan containing food, in a freezer bag. Insert an ordinary drinking straw in one corner of the bag opening. Seal the bag from one corner all the way to the straw in the other corner. Pinch the straw and corner of the bag tightly together to keep air from escaping, then suck out the excess air. When the air is removed, quickly pull out the straw and finish sealing the bag. This method works with bumpier foods like chicken parts, fish fillets, steaks, and chops. It also works well for freezing foods right in the serving dish, like a casserole or baked quiche. It is very important that you do not touch the straw to raw meats, into marinades or sauces, or into crumbs. Removing air bubbles from freezer bags is not as important as preventing food poisoning or choking!

Package your freezer bag foods in flat, thin layers. They freeze, thaw, and store more efficiently.

People often ask if they can re-use freezer bags. We only recommend that you re-use them if they have had dry ingredients like bread crumbs or chicken coating in them. Even if you wash them well you may not kill harmful bacteria that come from raw meats, eggs, or dairy products. You may also weaken the seams or the seal in the washing process.

If you are freezing foods that might puncture the bags, like sharp bones in chops, ribs, or steaks, consider double bagging them or using rigid plastic containers. Leaking bags are not fun!

A nine or ten inch pie or quiche dish will fit into most 1-gallon freezer bags. A 9x13x2 baking pan without handles will fit into a 2-gallon freezer bag as will many other shapes of baking dishes. Another use for freezer bags is to place each component of a recipe into a small food storage or freezer bag. Place the components of a meal into one larger labeled freezer bag to keep all the various parts together. This works well for casseroles or layered dishes that you wish to assemble after thawing.

You can thaw foods in freezer bags in the microwave if you use a low enough temperature that you do not melt the bags. Recipes with heavy cheese content can heat quickly and cause leaks in the freezer bags. Likewise, you can re-heat many foods stored in freezer bags. Just be very careful not to get the temperature too high. If the heat is high enough to actually *cook* in them, you may have a melted disaster.

Glass and ceramic dishes

Combined foods such as casseroles may be frozen in the dishes they will be cooked in and served from. When the food in the dish is cooled sufficiently, wrap it with freezer weight foil, freezer paper, or slide it into a freezer bag large enough to accommodate it. The main advantage of freezing in glass and ceramic is that you can freeze, defrost, bake and refrigerate in the same container. This is very convenient and cost effective. Glass and ceramic containers may be obtained in the usual retail stores, but be sure to check out garage sales, second hand stores, and your mother's cabinets and garage also.

Do not place a freezing glass or ceramic dish in a hot oven. You will risk a shattered dish if you do! If you happen to break or crack a glass dish containing food, please do yourself a favor and throw the whole thing out. Do not take chances with glass slivers!

Disposable or re-usable metal or foil pans

Follow the same wrapping instructions as with glass and ceramic dishes. The main disadvantage of foil pans is that they are generally fairly flimsy and may not stack up well until completely and firmly frozen. They also tend to scorch easily on the bottom because they are so thin. You will need to lower the cooking temperature 25 to 50 degrees to ensure even cooking. Another thing to remember about aluminum is that it has a chemical reaction when it comes into contact with highly acidic foods like tomato sauce and vinegar. You may not want to freeze lasagna or Italian casseroles in aluminum - the flavor may be affected, and the pan may even be damaged.

If you like the idea of freezing foods in metal, glass or ceramic dishes, but do not have very many of them, here is an option you might like to consider. Line your baking dishes with good quality plastic wrap or foil so that a few inches hang off the edges of the dish. Assemble your cooled recipe ingredients on top of the wrap. Place the assembled recipe on a level surface in the freezer and allow it to freeze until the food is firm to the touch. Remove the dish from the freezer and set it on a counter. Grasp the wrap with your hands and pop the firm block of food out of the dish. Either finish wrapping the food with more plastic wrap or foil, or place it inside a freezer bag. If you have difficulty removing the food from the dish, turn the dish upside down and run it under warm water until it is loosened enough to come out.

There are as many freezer container options as there are foods that will freeze. Experiment a little and find the combination of containers that works best for you.

Freezing in serving dishes is very convenient.

Lining your pans with foil allows you to freeze and remove blocks of food from a pan for easy freezing.

-22-

WORKSHEET B
Recipe Worksheet

Recipe: *Cheeseburger Quiche*

Meals:

	1	2	3	4	5	6

Serves: 6

Ingredients:

	1	2	3	4	5	6
Pie shell, unbaked	1	2	3	4	5	6
Browned ground beef	2 ½ C.	5 C.	7 ½ C.	10 C.	12 ½ C.	15 C.
Mayonnaise	½ C.	1 C.	1 ½ C.	2 C.	2 ½ C.	3 C.
Milk	½ C.	1 C.	1 ½ C.	2 C.	2 ½ C.	3 C.
Diced onion	2 T.	¼ C.	¼ C.+2T.	½ C.	½ C.+ 2T.	¾ C.
Eggs	2	4	6	8	10	12
Cornstarch	1 T.	2 T.	3 T.	4 T.	5 T.	6 T.
Shredded cheese	1 ½ C.	3 C.	4 ½ C.	6 C.	7 ½ C.	9 C.

Containers: Quiche pans, pie pans, 1-gallon freezer bags for filling only, 2-gallon bags for whole quiche

Assembly Directions:

In a mixing bowl blend mayonnaise, milk, eggs, and cornstarch. Distribute beef, onion, and cheese into Pie shells or into freezer bags. Pour egg mixture into pie shells or into 1-gallon freezer bags.

Freezing and Cooking Directions:

To pre-bake before freezing, preheat oven to 350°. Bake 35-40 minutes or until a knife inserted in the center comes out wet but clean. Cool, then wrap and freeze. To freeze mixture in bags, keep pie shells on hand in freezer. Seal quiche filling in freezer bags and freeze. To serve pre-baked quiche, thaw it, then warm up in 300° oven for 20 min. If quiche filling is frozen in a bag, thaw the mixture, pour it into unbaked pie shell, Bake in a preheated 350° oven for 35-40 minutes.

Comments:

Purchased OR homemade pie shells work fine. Fat free or regular mayo both work well. Sausage, ham, or bacon can be substituted for burger. Cheddar or Swiss work best and can be cut by ½ or ¼ and be fine.

STEP 3

Plan healthy options. We call this "Health by Stealth".

We have found that planning for Assembly Day is a great time to try to boost the nutritional quality of our meals. In the past, we found it very difficult to make consistently healthful meal decisions on a daily basis. We seemed to not have the right ingredients on hand, or not have time to incorporate a healthier food ingredient for our everyday one. To ask ourselves "what can I do to make this recipe higher in fiber, lower in fat, sodium and cholesterol, higher in vitamins and minerals?" meal after meal was very tiresome and we soon gave up in varying degrees.

Now we make all of those healthy meal plans and ingredient substitutions long in advance of when those foods will be eaten. We plan for any changes when we incorporate a new recipe into our menu and plan our shopping accordingly.

Nanci wanted her family to eat in a more healthy way, but was not sure how to begin. She thought she would have to call a family meeting and make a special announcement such as, " I am your mother. I love you so much that I want you to eat healthy foods. From this day forward we will not eat the way we are used to. Everything will be different from now on! We will eat more fruits and vegetables, less red meat and sugar. Someday you will all thank me for this." She hoped she would receive a round of applause, pats on the back and "Thanks Mom! We are so lucky to have a mother like you!" Tara persuaded her that it would not likely happen that way.

Most people, especially children and picky eaters of all ages, will balk at changes from the ordinary. Tara had learned years earlier that being sneaky was a more efficient way to get better nutrition not only on the table, but in the tummies of those you love. The number one rule is, "Never, *EVER*, tell anyone what you are up to! If you do, they will look suspiciously at every food brought to the table and clamp their lips shut until they turn purple! Tara convinced Nanci that starting with small, unnoticeable changes was preferable to an all-out wrestling match at the dinner table.

Nanci began putting just a little bit of cooked brown rice in with her instant white rice. She kept increasing the ratio of brown to white rice patiently and consistently over the next couple of years. Now Nanci can serve a bowl of brown rice at the table and everyone will help themselves! She used the same trick to get her family to eat a little bit of whole wheat pastas too!

We also found that we could puree many vegetables and hide them in our foods. Stirred into a sauce, casserole, soup, or meatloaf, green peppers will look like parsley flakes or crumbled oregano after running them through a food processor or blender. Pureed red peppers will absolutely disappear into anything red, like spaghetti sauce, sloppy joes, barbecued pork, or chili. Lightly cooked and pureed carrots will blend into anything red. Freshly pureed mushrooms will hide in any cooked meat recipe. We put this mushroom "paste" in meatballs, meatloaf, and meat patties.

This handy food processor helps us "sneak" nutrition in on the kids.

The trick is to start small and keep it a secret! If you put too great a quantity of a vegetable in a recipe, it may have too strong an aroma or flavor to keep it hidden. No one wants carrot sauce on their pasta! If your loved ones guess what you have done, they will never trust you again!

Sneaking like this is best done on Assembly Day when the kitchen is piled with foods. Daily cooks can try this, but if a picky eater sees a pepper or carrot out at 5 p.m., he knows that it is destined to be in his dinner somewhere! He will go "on the hunt" until he finds it. Of course, our kids see veggie chunks in spaghetti elsewhere. But if our children ask if there are any "weird things" in the food WE serve, we just say "**Do you see any?**"

STEP 3

PLAN YOUR SHOPPING

Fill out the Tally Sheet - (*Worksheet C*)
Use the sample tally sheet below as a guide. Finalize your list of recipes and write them in the left hand column of Worksheet C. Follow the directions on the cover of the blank *Tally Sheet* on page 41 in the *Worksheets Section* to fill out the form. Filling out this form will give you a complete list of all ingredients and other essentials you will need on Assembly Day.

Worksheet C Sample

Recipe Title	Meals For Cook #1	Meals For Cook #2	Ground Beef Fresh	Ground Beef Frozen	Chuck Roast	Boneless Breast	Chicken Parts	Cooked Diced	Whole Turkey	Ground Turkey	Turkey Breast	Cooked Diced	Sausage	Ground Pork	Ham	Pork Sausage	Bacon	Roast	Frozen Fillets	Fresh Fillets	Eggs	Margarine	Butter	Sour Cream	Cheddar
1. Taco Rice	3	3	6#																						3#
2. Crock Pot Beef	3	3		15#																					
3. Parsley Parmesan Chicken	3	3				19#																			
4. Sausage Rice Bake	3	3											3#												
5. Chicken in Marinade	3	3				9#																			
6. Chicken Fingers	3	3				12#																			
7. Ham + Potato Casserole	2	2													3#						8T	14oz			
8. Turkey Divan	3	3							30#																
9. Pork BBQ	2	2																6#							
10. Cheese-filled Shells	2	2																							
11.																									
12.																									
	27	27																							
Total Needed			6#	15#		21#	19#		30#	3#			3#		6#										3#
(-) Total on Hand				5#	6#	0	0		11#	0			0		0										1#
(=) Total to Buy			1#	9#		21#	19#		19#	3#			3#		6#										2#

Recipe Title	Meals For Cook #1	Meals For Cook #2	Quick Brown Rice	Sandwich Rolls	Bread Crumbs	Stuffing Shells	Cornflake Cereal		Diced onions	Peas	Mushrooms	Hash browns	Broccoli Spears		Green Onions
1.a Taco Rice	3	3	4c						6c						
2.a Crock Pot Beef	3	3		48											
3.a Parsley Parmesan Chicken	3	3			2c										
4.a Sausage Rice Bake	3	3	12c						9c	48oz	27oz				
5.a Chicken in marinade	3	3													
6.a Chicken Fingers	3	3			6c										
7.a Ham + Potato Casserole	2	2				24oz						8#			1⅓c
8.a Turkey Divan	3	3	9c										120oz		
9.a Pork BBQ	2	2							2c						
10.a Cheese-filled Shells	2	2				24oz									
11.a															
12.a															
	27	27													
Total Needed			25c	48	8c	24oz	24oz		11c	48	27oz	8#	120oz		1⅓c
(-) Total on Hand			25c	0	6c	0	0		11c	0	10oz	4#	0		0
(=) Total to Buy			0	48	2c	24oz	24oz		0	48	17oz	4#	120oz		1⅓c

STEP 3

Fill out the Shopping List (*Worksheet D*)

Transfer the ingredients and numbers from the "Total Needed" line on the Tally Sheet (*Worksheet C*) to the appropriate columns on your Shopping List (*Worksheet D*).

Tips to Plan Your Shopping:

1. Write in the total pounds, ounces, cups, etc. of each item. For example, canned whole tomatoes are sold by the ounce. Rather than writing " *6/28 ounce cans*", write "*whole canned tomatoes/168 oz.*" By doing this, you might see that you can buy one food service size can, meaning less time with the can opener. Take a hand-held calculator with you when you shop for making handy conversions.
2. Use the Equivalency Charts on pages 126-128 to assist you in figuring totals.
3. In the miscellaneous column, include such things as freezer bags, foil, freezer labels, rubber gloves, trash bags, permanent markers, dish soap, and snacks and lunch for Assembly Day.
4. Check your grocery advertisements and decide where to get what. It really pays to shop around, especially when buying large quantities. In our area, at least one of the chain stores is usually running chicken and beef on sale. Some stores have a price-matching policy which could save you time also.
5. You may use a different shopping list for each store you will visit, or use one list and highlight each store's specials with a different color. If you are splitting the shopping chores with a cooking partner, be very careful not to overlap ingredients on your lists, or you will buy more than you need!
6. Check to see if there is a food buying club in your area. Food buying clubs generally purchase foods from a cooperative warehouse that will take orders for bulk and retail pack foods and sell them at very good prices. We feel that we save *TONS* of money this way. Food buying clubs often make very good quality healthy food ingredients available and affordable to all. For more information on food buying clubs and cooperative buying, see page 139 in the *Appendix*.
7. When you know what quantities you need, call the supermarket meat counter well in advance and ask about quantity discounts, limits, and bulk packaging.
8. The meat department will also grind special meats for you, mix different ground meats together thoroughly, slice large cuts, cube steaks and do many other helpful things. Just ask early enough to give them adequate time to fill your order.
9. You can buy jars of chopped, minced, or pureed garlic in the produce section of your grocery store. This will save you a lot of "clove crushing".
10. Buy frozen diced onions in the frozen vegetable case in the supermarket. This will spare you a lot of tears!

Worksheet D Sample

Beef	Canned foods	Frozen Foods	Oils
Fresh ground, 7 lbs.	Tomato sauce, 132 oz.	Broccoli cuts, 2 lbs.	Canola oil, 12 oz.
Stew beef, 6 lbs.	Tomato paste, 8 oz.	Carrots, 1 lb.	Olive oil 6 oz.
Chuck roast, 5 lbs.	Kidney beans, 2 lbs.	Peas, 20 oz.	
	Crushed garlic, 3 oz.	Sliced mushrooms, 10 oz.	
		Diced onions, 3 lbs.	
Chicken	**Grains**	**Fresh Produce**	**Mixes**
Fresh parts, 8 lbs.	Quick brown rice, 16 oz.	Broccoli, 4 lg. bunches	Taco season pkts., 4
Boneless breast, 4 lbs.	Wild rice, 8 oz.	Green onions, 2 bunches	Onion soup mix, 2
Thighs, 6 lbs.		Red sweet peppers, 3	
		Green peppers, 2	
Turkey	**Pasta**	**Spices**	**Staples**
Frozen breasts, 12 lbs.	Elbow macaroni, 12 oz.	Oregano, 1.5 oz.	Flour, 5 lbs.
	Spaghetti, 16 oz.	Thyme, 1 oz.	Red wine vinegar, 8 oz.

STEP 3

Plan Your Prep Work

Fill out the "What to Do Before Assembly Day" and "What To Bring On Assembly Day" sections on *Worksheet E*. Use the sample page below to help you decide who will need to complete which tasks before Assembly Day arrives.

Worksheet E Sample

What To Do Before Assembly Day

Cook # 1 Tara	Cook # 2 Nanci
Brown ground beef - 5 lbs.	Make 24 cups of white sauce
Dice all celery	Cook 2 lbs. pasta
Dice 3 lbs. of ham	Skin all chicken parts
Grind 2 lbs. of ham	Shred 1 lb. Swiss cheese
Cook all dry beans	Shred 1 lb. carrots
Steam all diced onions and celery	Cook 24 oz. brown rice
Start one crock pot meal the night before	Start one crock pot meal the night before

What To Bring On Assembly Day

Cook # 1 Tara	Cook # 2 Nanci
Large cookware	Large measuring cups
Long handled utensils	Cutting boards
Inventory and prepared foods	Inventory and prep work foods
Freezer bags	Freezer bags
Foil	Food processor
Crock pot	Crock pot
Newsprint	Coolers and cardboard boxes

Cooking poultry, browning ground meats, making crumb coating, and many other chores can be done 2-3 days before your Assembly Day.

STEP 4
GO SHOPPING

Before you go. . .
✓ Clean out your refrigerator and freezer. You will need as much room as possible for the many groceries you will be bringing home. You should not leave perishable ingredients at room temperature for more than two hours.
✓ Be sure you allow yourself enough time to get the job done. It's much easier to do it all at once than to go out 4 different times.

When to go. . .
✓ Although we stock up on non-perishable items all month long as we watch for sales, the perishable groceries and meats that you want to start with fresh should be purchased no more than 2 or 3 days before Assembly Day.
✓ Be sure to leave yourself enough time to get your prep work done. If you make the mistake (like we have) of not shopping until the evening before Assembly Day, then you end up being on your feet for what seems like 3 days straight!
✓ People may get a little impatient waiting for you to check out at the supermarket if you have massive amounts and it is at a peak sales time. Be extra considerate and shop during the "off" hours. Try shopping during early morning, early afternoon, or late evening - anything to avoid the "rush hours".

What to take. . .
Wear comfortable clothing and take the following:
✓ Tally Sheet (*Worksheet C*)
✓ Shopping List (*Worksheet D*)
✓ Coolers during warm weather
✓ Adequate cash and checks
✓ Calculator
✓ Store advertisements
✓ Extra bags and boxes

What to Leave at home...
✓ Children (if at all possible)
✓ Pets (at any cost)

Usually, one of us shops while the other one stays with all of the children. Each of us thinks she got the better deal!

Nanci LOVES to shop and get the best bargains!

More Shopping Day Tips:
✓ Buying your food items in large quantities may save you some money and the time it takes finding storage, opening, using, and throwing away many small cans or jars. We look for items like Worcestershire sauce, vinegar, soy sauce, and cooking oil in 1-gallon containers.
✓ Look for freezer labels near the freezer containers and wraps in large supermarkets and discount stores.
✓ Try to shop at places where you can bag your own groceries. Yes, this is extra work, but we have a good reason for it. Each cook has her own "to do" list before Assembly Day. Having each cook's ingredients in separated bags or boxes is very helpful.
✓ Grocers will sometimes waive the limits on advertised specials if you order large quantities and call 3-4 days in advance of when you need to pick them up.
✓ Sometimes the small independent grocers are the most willing to work with you!
✓ Try to put refrigerated and frozen items in your cart last, so they stay cold longer.
✓ Be sure to check expiration dates.
✓ Don't purchase dented canned goods - they can be terribly hard to open.

STEP 5
PREPARE FOR ASSEMBLY DAY

We try to think of this project as a "cooking week". Of course, it doesn't take a whole week, but there are things that HAVE to be done ahead if this is going to work. Just remember, if you have chosen 8-10 recipes and make 3 of each, you will only be doing this once every 4 to 6 weeks and *IT WILL BE WORTH IT!* We think of cooking week in 4 processes - 1. Planning; 2. Shopping; 3. Prep Work; 4. Assembly Day. We've already covered the first 2 processes, so you are half way done!

Our rule for Prep Work is:
The more we get done before Assembly Day, the better!
We divide these pre-Assembly Day chores between us:
- ✓ Skin chicken parts
- ✓ Cook and drain pasta
- ✓ Make coatings for chicken parts
- ✓ Start crock pot meals
- ✓ Chop and steam vegetables
- ✓ Brown ground meats
- ✓ Dice or grind ham
- ✓ Make sauces
- ✓ Cook and dice poultry
- ✓ Soak and cook dry beans

AFTER the big shopping trip is no time to clean out the refrigerator. You'll need all the room you can get.

As we go we try to separate the items for each recipe into its own bag. For example, all the boneless skinless chicken breasts for the chicken fingers go into one bag, and all the boneless skinless chicken breasts for marinades go into another bag. This keeps us from using up too much chicken breast in the first recipe and not having enough for the next one.

To be honest, some Assembly Days we have started with very little of these things done. It made for a much longer Assembly Day, but it was better than not cooking at all.

It also helps to explain what you are about to embark on to your family and friends. They need to know that this will require a big time commitment from you, but that the results will be worth it. Go over your cooking week schedule with them and ask them to help you with tasks like carrying in groceries, caring for small children while dicing hot poultry, and helping with simple meal preparations while you do other important tasks to get ready for Assembly Day (it is okay to send them out to eat).

If you are traveling to a cooking partner's house:
- ✓ Put as much "stuff" in your vehicle the night before as possible.
- ✓ Post your copy of *Worksheet E* in a prominent place and check it frequently.
- ✓ Turn your freezer to its coldest temperature in readiness for the foods you will bring home.
- ✓ Arrange your freezer to accommodate the new foods.

If you are hosting the Assembly Day:
- ✓ Remove all unneeded items from your kitchen counters and work spaces.
- ✓ Empty out your trash and have a large empty trash container for each cook on hand.
- ✓ Set out your mixing bowls, pans, utensils, etc.
- ✓ Turn your freezer to its coldest temperature.
- ✓ Arrange your freezer to accommodate the new foods you will put into it.
- ✓ Line all work spaces with several layers of clean newsprint. This is a big help with clean-up tasks. as you drip or spill on it, just roll up that layer and discard it.

STEP 6
ASSEMBLE ENTREES & STOCK FREEZER

THE BIG DAY HAS FINALLY ARRIVED!

Here is a list of items we feel are necessary for Assembly Day:

Long handled utensils:
Forks
Slotted spoons
Ladles
Wire whisks
Tongs
Metal/Rubber spatulas

Large containers for mixing:
Dish pans with flat bottoms
Mixing bowls
Water bath canners

Cookware and bakeware:
Two large rimmed baking sheets
Two 9"x13"x2" baking pans
One or two 2-quart glass dishes
One paring knife
One chopping knife
One slicing knife
Two sets of standard measuring cups
Two sets of standard measuring spoons
One deep, covered pan or one stock pot
One cutting board
One large 12" skillet with a lid
One 2-quart covered sauce pan
One colander (large strainer)
Two oven mitts
Two pot holders
One kitchen timer
One 2-cup glass measure

Items to accumulate gradually:
Microwaveable containers
Mixing bowls with handles and spouts
Extra kitchen timers
Electric hand mixer
Large, lidded containers for marinating
Electric stand mixer
Large-sized sets of measuring cups
Electric can opener
Electric skillets/hot plates
Food processor or blender
Spring mechanism cookie scoops
Crock pots
Large electric roasting pans
Large pastry brush
4-cup glass measure
Bulb baster

Each cook needs her/his own set of basic items but only use as many dishes as you are willing to wash!

These are the "can't-cook-without-'em" Assembly Day basics for Tara and Nanci

STEP 6

Assembly Day Procedures

We try hard to start by 9 a.m. and are usually still washing dishes in the evening. Many people using our system work faster than we do. On the IDEAL Assembly Day, we have no kids to watch, no lunch to fix, and nowhere to be that night. Our husbands take the kids out to dinner and then bring them home and put them to bed. Then they rub our feet and say, *"Honey, why don't you go soak in the tub while I finish cleaning up."* On REAL Assembly Days, we sometimes have one sick kid, nothing for lunch, and three evening meetings we are expected to attend. We just don't want you to get frustrated striving for perfection. No one has the perfect cooking partner, mate, kids, or schedule. Be flexible. You'll live longer!

✓ **Post a Meal Inventory Checklist** (*Worksheet F*) **in a prominent place.** A kitchen desk top or hanging clip is ideal.

✓ **Start assembling entrees.**
Our method is simple. One cook does the chicken, the other does the beef, and we share the rest. Each cook takes a recipe and checks the Tally Sheet (*Worksheet C*) to see how many of that recipe needs to be made. The cook follows the appropriate column on the recipe and begins assembling the ingredients for her own *AND* the other cooks entrees. Time is saved by stirring it all up at once! If the food is hot, it is cooled to room temperature or chilled in the refrigerator before it is packaged for the freezer.

Mixing in large quantities is one way to save time and energy on Assembly Day.

We ask the other cook how she wants each recipe packaged (pans, bags, rigid containers). In this way, each recipe is assembled, cooled, packaged, and frozen *as quickly as possible*. Besides the sense of accomplishment, the quality of the food is better because you have gotten it into the freezer as *quickly as possible*. The chances of cross-contamination from meats is also greatly reduced this way because each cook is not switching back and forth between raw meats.

We leave all the perishable ingredients in the refrigerator until they are needed. This may seem difficult when making large quantities, but we have dealt with it in a couple of different ways. In the winter, the world is your refrigerator! Put an indoor/outdoor thermometer on your porch or in your garage. If the temperature remains cool enough (32°F. to 35° F.), you can consider it a refrigerator. If the temperature remains 32°F. or below, you can consider it a freezer! We have also frozen water in sealed, 1 liter plastic drink bottles and used them as ice packs in a cooler. If you choose to use the frozen water method, make sure and leave adequate air space at the top of the bottle to leave room for the water to expand!

Assembly Day Tips

✓ Get Plenty of sleep the night before Assembly Day.

✓ Assemble and freeze soupy casseroles early in the day so you have a level surface to place them on.

✓ Start time consuming, slow cooking, or marinating foods early.

✓ Remember to assemble in large quantities. For example, do not assemble each quiche individually. Combine the ingredients for all of the quiche at the same time and distribute the ingredients equally. This will save lots of time!

✓ Think about which days are your busiest and pre-cook a few items for those days. They will only need a quick warm-up, not an extended baking time.

✓ Line baking sheets with foil between each batch of a recipe like broiled meatballs for easier clean-up. This frees up the pan for the next batch. Slide the foil with hot food off the pan onto several layers of newsprint to cool and the pan is ready to go again.

A cookie scoop makes quick work of meatballs.
The foil makes clean-up chores easier.

✓ Use as few pots, pans, and utensils as possible and wash well between recipes. This makes clean-up easier and forces you to wash your hands several times that day.

✓ Make sure you only put as much food in a freezer container as will be easily consumed. This will cut down on leftovers and food waste.

✓ Just a word of encouragement - the day will be half over before it seems like you get anything done!

✓ Wear good supportive shoes and exchange them with another pair halfway through the day.

✓ Tall kitchen stools allow you to sit and work at the same time.

✓ Play upbeat music to help you keep a good pace.

✓ Take a lunch break and put your feet up.

✓ Have a large trash can posted at each cook's designated spot! Keep conversations positive and uplifting. Gossip is destructive and your partner will tire of it quickly.

✓ Be clean! Please shower, wash your hair, and pull it back. No one enjoys hair in the food, especially if it belongs to your cooking partner!

✓ Let your answering machine or voice mail do its job. Answering the phone chews up too much time!

✓ Hire a babysitter for the children, or better yet, trade childcare with another 30 Day Gourmet!

✓ If children must be on the premises, keep them happy! Check out some new books and videos. Set up a self-serve snack table.

✓ Keep your beverages in sport drink cups that have lids, handles, and extra long straws. Food cannot fall into them, and the drink will not spill out if you knock it over. The handle keeps your hands away from your germs, and the food bacteria away from you!

✓ Wear an apron. Having a couple of pockets for your marking pen and labels is very handy.

✓ Cover all of your work surfaces with several sheets of clean newsprint to catch spills and drips.

✓ Enjoy a couple of snacks throughout the day to keep your energy level up.

✓ Remember to stop and admire your work occasionally. You are accomplishing great things!

STEP 6

Stocking the Freezer Tips

✓ Keep your freezer temperature at 0°F or colder and keep the door shut as much as possible!
✓ Label all foods clearly. Many foods look the same when frozen. When cooking with a partner, initial each container of food so they are easy to divide later.
✓ Don't try to freeze hot or warm foods. It will make your freezer work less efficiently and cause ice crystals to form all over your food.
✓ If you are the visiting cook, consider leaving at least part of your food in the host's freezer (if there is room) until it is frozen solid.
✓ If you have a chest freezer, don't put all of one kind of food in a layer. Stagger the foods so that you don't have to dig to the bottom to find what you want. If you do not distribute the foods well, you may get to the bottom of the freezer and discover that you are stuck eating the same recipe 3 times at the end of a month!
✓ If you have trouble getting your food to freeze quickly, you may be trying to put too much in at one time. Do not freeze more than 3 lbs. of fresh food per cubic foot of freezer space. In other words, do not freeze more than 30 pounds of new foods in a 10 cu. ft. freezer, or 45 pounds in a 15 cu. ft. freezer. A maximum of 60 pounds of freshly prepared foods should go into a 20 cu. ft. freezer. If you want to freeze more than is recommended, leave some of your foods in the refrigerator overnight and add them when the other food is frozen.

Consider placing one week's worth of recipes in a bag or box so that you eat the food in an orderly manner. This may sound silly, but we tend to eat the foods we like best within the first two weeks, and are left with our less favorites for the remainder of the month.
Remember to fill out your Meal Inventory Checklist *(Worksheet F)*

Yes – you really CAN fit 30 entrees in a standard refrigerator's freezer –
along with frozen juice, ice cubes, ice cream and more!

STEP 6

Fill out Meal Inventory Checklist *(Worksheet F)* as you put your labeled entrees into the freezer. If you make more than 18 recipes, use two inventory checklists. As you prepare your entrees for the freezer, fill in one of these checklists for each cook (sometimes you end up with more than you planned). Each cook should take the checklist home and put it on the freezer door (or some equally conspicuous place).

Directions: Place a slash mark in one box for each entree as it goes into the freezer (this way you can always know how many total entrees you have.) Fill in any ingredients that you will need to purchase or have on hand to serve with each entree. You may also make a note of an entree you need to save for a special occasion. As you remove an entree from the freezer to serve it, cross it off the list.

Worksheet F Sample

MEAL INVENTORY CHECKLIST Date_____							
# Of Recipes Stored						**Recipe**	**Needed on hand for serving**
/	/	X				Taco Rice	Shredded cheese, tortillas, sour cream, olives, fresh tomatoes
/	X	X				Crock Pot Beef	Sandwich buns, condiments
/	X	X				Parsley Parmesan Chicken	
/	X					Sausage Rice Bake	Grated parmesan cheese
/	/	X				Chicken in Deb's Marinade	
/	/					Chicken Fingers	
/	/	X				Ham and Potato Casserole	Cornflake topping, butter
/	X					Turkey Divan	Frozen in components to be assembled after thawing.
X	X					Pork BBQ	Sandwich buns <u>Serve at picnic on 5th</u>
/	X					Cheese-Filled Shells	Spaghetti or marinara sauce, grated parmesan cheese

STEP 7
CLEAN UP AND EVALUATE

For us, whichever cook finishes her final recipe earliest begins to clean up while the other is finishing her last recipe. It may take longer than you think, especially if you have not lined your work surfaces with newsprint or limited yourself on the amount of cookware you used. You will be glad if you were diligent in washing your dishes between recipes! At this point, your feet will probably be aching and you'll be a bit slap-happy, but knowing that you have so much food prepared and stashed in your freezer will feel great! Don't be surprised if you do not want to eat them for a few days and keep opening up your freezer door just to marvel at them!

As far as trash is concerned, we keep any plastic cottage cheese cartons, ricotta cheese tubs, margarine tubs, etc. to put discarded grease, meat drippings, poultry skin and bones in. This makes leaking trash bags a little less of a problem. In regards to recycling, we are all for it! The problem is that on Assembly Day you will really slow yourself down by soaking labels off bottles, crushing cans, and rinsing out cartons. Our secret is to throw them in the trash - then wait until your spouse comes home. If he is a truly dedicated recycler, he will dig through the trash and wash them out - works at Tara's house anyway!!!

We try to do a quick evaluation of what went right and wrong. How did it go? What will you do differently next time? Writing your observations on paper will really help you for your next Assembly Day. Be sure to write changes you would like to make on the recipes also. Save your worksheets from each of your cooking adventures. You'll be surprised at how handy this information will be later on.

We recommend that you read through the planning section occasionally to remind you of procedures and tips. You may discover some helpful information that you missed the first time through! Make sure to check out the Appendix section of this book for helpful information on food safety, safe thawing practices, and much, much more helpful information.

By now, if you have stayed on course, you have planned, shopped, prepared, assembled, packaged, labeled and frozen a bunch of great foods for your freezer. Whew! Take a deep breath and relax. Tomorrow you will begin to enjoy all the benefits of being a 30 Day Gourmet.

That's it! You're done! Congratulations and welcome to 30 Day Gourmet cooking!

Make Assembly Day a party!

This is your celebration of not having to make dinner for a very, very LONG time!

MENU PLANNER CALENDAR SAMPLE

We have included this calendar to aid you in daily meal planning. Fill in the dates on this calendar and make notes of what you want to serve on the especially busy days. Also make note of when you will have company and what you plan to serve. Mark vacations and any frozen entrees you would like to take along. Filling these events in BEFORE you even choose your recipes would be especially helpful. If you fill in the side dishes you plan to serve with each entree, grocery shopping will be even easier and more efficient.

Worksheet G Sample

Sunday	Monday	Tuesday	Wednesday	Thursday	Friday	Saturday
	Ballet at 4:30 Chicken Fingers Make ahead Mashed Potatoes Jell-O and carrots	Soccer at 4:30 Taco Rice Salad Peaches	Choir at 7:00 Beef Sandwiches Buns Oven fries Green beans	Soccer at 4:00 Turkey & Noodles Carrot salad Fruit slush	Swiss Steak Baked Potatoes Broccoli Canned pears	Lasagna Spinach salad Breadsticks Fruit salad
Church 7:00 Baked Chicken Stir fry veggies Frozen salad Cookies	Ballet at 4:30 Burgers Home fries Slaw Apple salad	Soccer at 4:30 Pizza Dinner W/team in town	Choir at 7:00 Ham Loaf Dressing Sweet Potatoes	Soccer at 4:00 Tetrazzini Broccoli salad Orange salad	Grilled Chicken Corn Grilled veggies	Soccer game Meatloaf Potato hash Fruit slush
Church 7:00 Company Savory Baked Chicken Spinach salad	Ballet at 4:30 Pork BBQ Sand. Buns, Corn Broccoli	Soccer at 4:30 Spaghetti Salad Garlic bread	Choir at 7:00 Shepherd's Pie Sautéed apples	Soccer at 4:00 Turkey Noodles Carrot salad Peaches Cottage cheese	Birthday dinner Eat at Mom's	Soccer game Sausage Rice Sauteed apples Steamed carrots
Church 7:00 Swiss Steak Mashed Potatoes Broccoli casserole	Ballet at 4:30 W. Country Cod Wild rice dress. Stir fry veggies	Soccer at 4:30 Hungarian Stew Sour Dough rolls Peas	Choir at 7:00 Ham Loaf Crispy Potatoes Asparagus	Soccer at 4:00 Roasted Turkey Mashed Potatoes Gravy Dressing	Medit. Chicken Mixed vegetables Garlic biscuits Apple sauce	Soccer game Team cookout
Church 7:00 Grilled Chicken Roasted Potatoes Grilled veggies	Ballet at 4:30 Dinner at Mom's Bring dessert	Soccer at 4:30 Broiled Chicken Stir fry veggies Rice Fruit salad	Choir at 7:00 Cheese Shells French bread Tossed salad			

This calendar would also be very helpful if boring lunches And helter skelter breakfasts are problems for you. Check out our *Month of Breakfast and Lunch Ideas* on page 138. You could plan a two week rotation so that all you have to do is look at the calendar. No decision-making early in the morning, and you won't eat the same thing day after day.

PLANNING WORKSHEETS

■ You will use these each time you cook so keep this set as master copies.

■ We suggest that you copy 5-10 of each at a time. You know how quickly a month can fly by.

■ Please ONLY make copies for yourself. When your friends start begging for your organizational secrets, give them our toll free number or address. Thanks!

WORKSHEET A

ON-HAND INVENTORY LIST			
ITEM NAME	QUANTITY	STORAGE PLACE	VALUE

WORKSHEET B
Recipe Worksheet

Recipe_____

Meals: 1   2   3   4   5   6
Serves_____

Ingredients:

_____ _____ _____ _____ _____ _____ _____
_____ _____ _____ _____ _____ _____ _____
_____ _____ _____ _____ _____ _____ _____
_____ _____ _____ _____ _____ _____ _____
_____ _____ _____ _____ _____ _____ _____
_____ _____ _____ _____ _____ _____ _____
_____ _____ _____ _____ _____ _____ _____
_____ _____ _____ _____ _____ _____ _____
_____ _____ _____ _____ _____ _____ _____
_____ _____ _____ _____ _____ _____ _____
_____ _____ _____ _____ _____ _____ _____
_____ _____ _____ _____ _____ _____ _____
_____ _____ _____ _____ _____ _____ _____
_____ _____ _____ _____ _____ _____ _____

Containers: _____

Assembly Directions:

_____
_____
_____
_____
_____
_____

Freezing and Cooking Directions:

_____
_____
_____
_____
_____

Comments:

WORKSHEET C
TALLY SHEET

Directions:

1. Write the name of your first recipe on line 1 and line 1a. Fill in how many meals of each recipe you will need for each cook.

2. In the diagonal columns, fill in the needed ingredients. Going horizontally across lines 1 and 1a, fill in the appropriate amounts of each ingredient.

3. Write down the name of your next recipe on lines 2 and 2a. Again going across the Tally Sheet, write in the appropriate ingredients and the amounts of each. Do the same for all your recipes. Be sure to account for any freezer bags, spray oils, etc... needed for your recipes on your Assembly Day.

4. After ALL of your recipe ingredients have been accounted for, going down the chart vertically, tally the TOTAL AMOUNT NEEDED of each ingredient. For example; total all the ground beef and put that number in the "total needed" box under ground beef. Total all the boneless chicken breasts needed and place that number in the "total needed" box under boneless chicken breast. Make sure to take into account whether the meats must be fresh, or can start from frozen.

5. Get out the On-Hand Inventory List *(Worksheet A)* that each cook brings to the planning session. Cross off the items you already have and write the amounts of them onto your list of What To Bring On Assembly Day *(Worksheet E)*. This eliminates the guesswork of who promised to bring the rice or oregano.

6. Refer back to the Tally Sheet *(Worksheet C)*. In the "total on hand" box, subtract the ingredients that each of you will be bringing to Assembly Day. (refer to *Worksheet A*) and write in your totals.

7. Continue on with the steps for the Shopping List *(Worksheet D)*

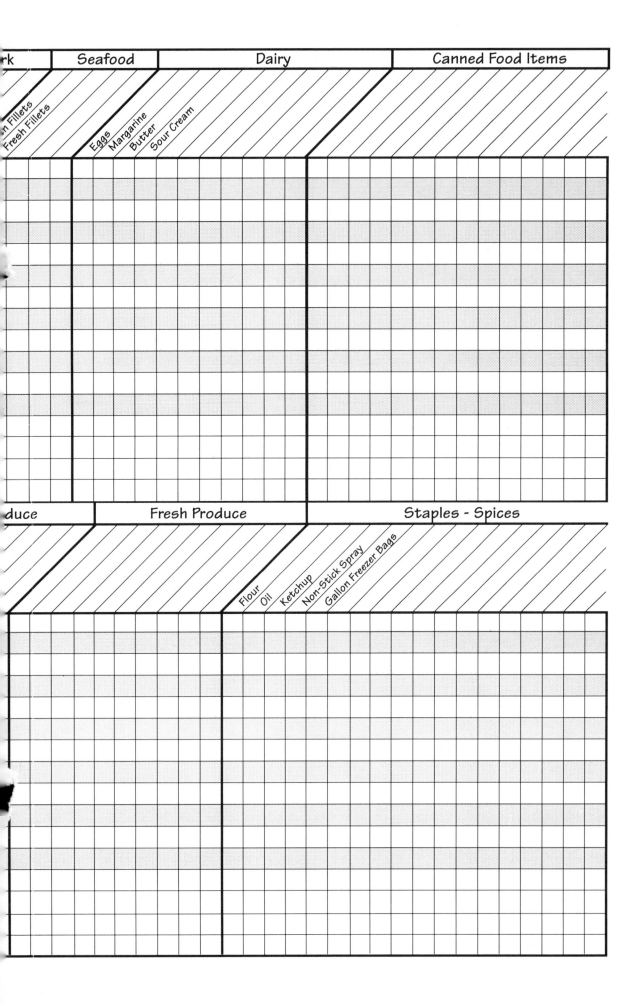

rk	Seafood		Dairy				Canned Food Items

n Fillets / Fresh Fillets

Eggs / Margarine / Butter / Sour Cream

duce	Fresh Produce		Staples - Spices

Flour / Oil / Ketchup / Non-Stick Spray / Gallon Freezer Bags

| Recipe Title | Meals For Cook #1 | Meals For Cook #2 | Food Type | | | Beef | | | Chicken | | | Turkey | | | Po |
			Ground Beef Fresh	Ground Beef Frozen		Boneless Breast	Chicken Parts	Cooked Diced	Whole Turkey	Ground Turkey	Turkey Breast	Cooked Diced	Ground Pork	Ham	Pork Sausage	Bacon	Froz
1.																	
2.																	
3.																	
4.																	
5.																	
6.																	
7.																	
8.																	
9.																	
10.																	
11.																	
12.																	
Total Needed																	
(-) Total on Hand																	
(=) Total to Buy																	

Recipe Title	Meals For Cook #1	Meals For Cook #2	Food Type	Grains, Pasta, Dry Beans, Breads, Crumb Crackers				Frozen Pro
1.a								
2.a								
3.a								
4.a								
5.a								
6.a								
7.a								
8.a								
9.a								
10.a								
11.a								
12.a								
Total Needed								
(-) Total on Hand								
(=) Total to Buy								

WORKSHEET D
SHOPPING LIST

BEEF	CANNED GOODS	FROZEN FOODS	OILS
CHICKEN			MIXES
TURKEY		FRESH PRODUCE	STAPLES
PORK	GRAINS		
FISH	PASTA		
DAIRY	BREADS	SPICES	MISCELLANEOUS
	DRY BEANS		

WORKSHEET E
WHAT TO DO AND BRING

What To Do Before Assembly Day

Cook #1	Cook #2

What To Bring On Assembly Day

Cook # 1	Cook #2

WORKSHEET F

Meal Inventory Checklist							
Date_____							

# Of Recipes Stored						Recipe	Needed On Hand For Serving

Be sure to place a slash in a box as a recipe goes into the freezer, then cross one off as it comes out to be served. You can use this list for foods other than your **30 Day Gourmet** recipes to help you keep track of what might be lurking in the back corner!

WORKSHEET G (OPTIONAL)

MONTHLY MENU PLANNER   **MONTH/YEAR**_____

Saturday					
Friday					
Thursday					
Wednesday					
Tuesday					
Monday					
Sunday					

BEEF ENTREES

Taco Rice

Crock Pot Beef Sandwiches

Zippy Spaghetti Sauce

Lazy Day Lasagna

Hungarian Stew

Master Meat Mix

Meatloaf & Meatballs

Meatloaf & Meatball Sauces

■ Swiss Steak

■ Shepherd's Pie

■ Sloppy Joe Casserole

■ Marinade for Beef

■ Master Beef Cube Mix & Sauce

■ Cowboy Stew

■ Beef Stroganoff

TIPS FOR BEEF ENTREES

General Tips For Beef
✓ One pound of fresh ground beef will yield approximately 2-1/2 to 3 cups of browned beef.
✓ 1/4 pound of fresh beef is considered to be a standard serving. Adjust the portions you freeze to fit your family's needs.
✓ We use a cookie scoop with a spring mechanism to form meatballs. Much quicker!
✓ Remember, if you buy ahead and freeze beef, you should cook it thoroughly before re-freezing. For example, frozen ground beef can be thawed, browned, then used in a recipe like *Sloppy Joe Casserole*, then frozen. If you want to use the frozen ground beef for a meatloaf, meatballs, or patties, it must be thoroughly cooked (no pink in the center) before re-freezing.
✓ When purchasing beef from the supermarket, avoid the leaking packages and place the beef on the bottom of the cart so that if there are meat juice drips, they don't drip on your other foods!
✓ If you are thawing foods that need to be reheated, heat them thoroughly to a temperature of 165°F or until hot and steaming. Thawed soups and gravies should be brought to a rolling boil before serving.
✓ Purchase a meat thermometer and become familiar with its use. Save the directions for review.
✓ Ground beef should be heated to a temperature of at least 160° F to be considered safe to eat, no matter what kind of dish it is in or how it is prepared. Thoroughly cooked ground beef will have no pink left in the middle or in juices.
✓ For beef or veal roasts, steaks, or chops, 145° F is considered medium rare, 160° F is considered medium, and 170° F is considered well done.
✓ Not sure if you have kept something in the refrigerator too long? When in doubt, throw it out! Never taste food that looks or smells strange! It is better to just discard it!
✓ Purchase beef that is as fresh as possible. The quality will not improve in the freezer, so start with the best quality you can afford.
✓ Remember to cool your cooked meats before you freeze them.
✓ For the best quality and safety of your freezer meals, do not freeze more than 3 pounds of fresh foods per cubic foot of freezer space at one time.

Healthy Tips For Beef
✓ Try rinsing the fat off your cooked ground beef. Place the hot, cooked ground meat in a colander in your sink with a pan under the colander. Catch all possible fat in the pan and discard. After the meat has drained, pour hot water over the meat in the colander to remove remaining surface fat. Continue to run the hot water so that the fat runs through your drain easily and does not clog in the pipes. Allow the water to drain well from the beef before using it.

✓ To lighten up your beef, try soaking 1/3 cup of dry bulger in broth or water. It will measure about 2/3 cup when soaked. Add your 2/3 cup of soaked bulger to 1/2 pound of ground beef. This will work in patties, meatballs, and loaves.

✓ You can add 1/2 cup of cooked, mashed black beans to 1/2 pound of ground beef. Try this in patties, loaves, and meatballs.

✓ A good fat and cholesterol reducer is to use a product called Texturized Vegetable Protein (TVP). Try using it as a complete or partial beef substitute. This product can be purchased at health food stores or through food cooperatives (see page 139 for more information). It comes in small rice sized pieces, that when re-constituted with broth or water, look like cooked ground beef. This is a very high protein, low fat and economical substitute. 2-1/2 cups of reconstituted TVP is equal to one pound of fresh ground beef, or 2-1/2 cups of cooked ground beef. If you fear the reactions of the people you serve, try mixing 1/4 TVP to 3/4 beef - this is usually a good way to begin.

✓ When determining how high the percentage of fat you want in your ground beef, consider that 73% lean will yield moist, juicy cooked meat. Recipes made with 80% lean ground beef will be juicy, firm, and have great flavor. 93% lean meat will be compact, drier, and very firm when cooked.

Recipe: Taco Rice

Meals:	1	2	3	4	5	6
serves 4-6						
Ingredients:						
ground beef, chicken or turkey (uncooked)	1 lb.	2 lbs.	3 lbs.	4 lbs.	5 lbs.	6 lbs.
onion, diced	1 C.	2 C.	3 C.	4 C.	5 C.	6 C.
taco seasoning packet	1	2	3	4	5	6
canned tomatoes	16 oz.	32 oz.	48 oz.	64 oz.	80 oz.	96 oz.
white or brown rice, (cooked measurement)	2 C.	4 C.	6 C.	8 C.	10 C.	12 C.
cheese, shredded	2 C.	4 C.	6 C.	8 C.	10 C.	12 C.

Containers: Freezer bags or containers suitable for your family. We often do some small (for snacks) and some large (for meals).

Assembly Directions:
Brown meat and drain. Combine meat, onion, taco seasoning packet(s), cooked rice and tomatoes in saucepan. Simmer until thick - about 30 minutes.

Freezing and Cooking Directions:
Cool, label, and freeze in bags or rigid containers. Also freeze a ziptop bag with 2 C. of shredded cheese for each meal. **To serve,** thaw completely. For taco salad, warm over medium heat. Serve with lettuce, taco chips, tomatoes, sour cream and the enclosed cheese.

Comments:
This stuff is great! We use it for main entrees and snacks to fill taco shells or to fill flour tortillas for burritos. Melted cheese on top of corn chips and Taco Rice makes yummy nachos.

Recipe: Crock Pot Beef Sandwiches

Serves:	6	12	18	24	30	36
Ingredients:						
beef roast, chuck roast or thick chuck steak, fat trimmed and discarded	2-1/2 lbs.	5 lbs.	7-1/2 lbs.	10 lbs.	12-1/2 lbs.	15 lbs.
dry Italian or Ranch salad dressing packets or onion soup mix packets	2	4	6	8	10	12
water	1 C.	2 C.	3 C.	4 C.	5 C.	6 C.
On Hand:						
buns or hoagie rolls	8	16	24	32	40	48

Containers: quart size ziptop freezer bags or 2-1/2 C. rigid freezer containers

Assembly Directions:
In a cold crock pot, place the thawed or fresh roast. Pour the contents of the salad dressing or soup packets over the meat. Pour the water over all. Cover crock pot with lid. Can be cooked overnight on low heat or 6 hours on high heat until meat shreds easily with a fork. When done, turn off crock pot and uncover it to cool quickly.
If you wish, the filling is now ready to eat. Follow the serving directions below.

Freezing and Cooking Directions:
When cooled, place meat and juice in a freezer bag or container. Seal, label and freeze. (2 cups fills 8 average sized buns.)
To serve, thaw and heat in a microwave or saucepan over medium heat until warmed through. Serve over rolls or in buns.

Comments:
Roasts over 7-1/2 lbs. may not fit well in a crock pot. Try to borrow an extra crock pot if you choose to make more than 7-1/2 lbs.
This is a large recipe and we divide each recipe in half for freezing purposes. About 1/4-1/3 C of cooked meat is a serving.
Barbecue Option: *Reduce water by half. Pour water and 1 C. of barbecue sauce per recipe over all. (May add more barbecue sauce later to taste.)*

Recipe: Zippy Spaghetti Sauce

Meals: serves 4-6	1	2	3	4	5	6
Ingredients:						
ground beef, uncooked	1 lb.	2 lbs.	3 lbs.	4 lbs.	5 lbs.	6 lbs.
onion, diced	1/2 C.	1 C.	1-1/2C.	2 C.	2-1/2C.	3 C.
garlic, minced	2t.	1T.+1t.	2 T.	2T.+2t.	3T.+1t.	4 T.
green pepper, minced (optional)	1/2 C.	1 C.	1-1/2C.	2 C.	2-1/2C.	3 C.
tomato sauce	8 oz.	16 oz.	24 oz.	32 oz.	40 oz.	48 oz.
tomato paste	6 oz.	12 oz.	18 oz.	24 oz.	30 oz.	36 oz.
water	1 C.	2 C.	3 C.	4 C.	5 C.	6 C.
oregano	1 t.	2 t.	1 T.	1T.+1t.	1T.+2t.	2 T.
basil	1/4 t.	1/2 t.	3/4 t.	1 t.	1-1/4t.	1-1/2t.
sugar (optional)	1 t.	2 t.	1 T.	1T.+1t.	1T.+2t.	2 T.
pepper	1/4 t.	1/2 t.	3/4 t.	1 t.	1-1/4t.	1-1/2t.

Containers: 1-gallon freezer bags or 6-cup freezer containers
Assembly Directions:
Brown beef and drain. Combine with remaining ingredients in a saucepan or crock pot. Simmer one hour in saucepan or 6 hours to overnight in crock pot. Cool completely. The longer this sauce simmers, the thicker it gets.

Freezing and Cooking Directions:
Pour cooled sauce into freezer bags or freezer containers. Label and freeze. Before serving, thaw completely. Heat in a saucepan over medium heat or in microwave.

Comments:
We use this for spaghetti, lasagna, goulash, manicotti, cheese-filled shells and *pizza casserole among other things. The hardest part of all these meals is having the sauce made.
__Pizza Casserole__: Nanci's kids love this! Just spread 32 oz (4 cups) of sauce in the bottom of a 9x13 pan. Sprinkle 2 C. of shredded cheddar or mozzarella cheese over sauce. Place 2 cans of refrigerator biscuits (20) on top. Bake at 350° for 30 minutes.

Recipe: Lazy Day Lasagna

Meals:	**1**	**2**	**3**	**4**	**5**	**6**
serves 6						
Ingredients:						
cottage cheese	12 oz.	24 oz.	36 oz.	48 oz.	60 oz.	72 oz.
mozzarella cheese, shredded	2 C. (8 oz.)	4 C. (16 oz.)	6 C. (24 oz.)	8 C. (32 oz.)	10 C. (40 oz.)	12 C. (48 oz.)
eggs	2	4	6	8	10	12
parsley, chopped	1/3 C.	2/3 C.	1 C.	1-1/3C.	1-2/3C.	2 C.
onion powder	1 t.	2 t.	1 T.	1T.+1t.	1T.+2t.	2 T.
dried basil leaves	1/2 t.	1 t.	1-1/2t.	2 t.	2-1/2t.	1 T.
pepper	1/8 t.	1/4 t.	1/4 t.	1/2 t.	1/2 t.	3/4 t.
*spaghetti sauce (homemade or purchased)	32 oz.	64 oz.	96 oz.	128 oz.	160 oz.	192 oz.
ground beef or ground turkey, cooked	3/4 C.	1-1/2C.	2-1/4C.	3 C.	3-3/4C.	4-1/2C.
lasagna noodles, regular, uncooked	9	18	27	36	45	54
**water; more or less	3/4 C.	1-1/2C.	2-1/4C.	3 C.	3-3/4C.	4-1/2C.

On Hand: grated parmesan cheese
Containers: 12x8x2 baking dish

Assembly Directions:

In large bowl, mix cheeses, eggs, parsley, onion powder, basil, and pepper until well blended; set aside.
In medium bowl, mix together spaghetti sauce and cooked ground beef.
In 12x8x2 baking dish, spread 3/4 C. meat sauce. Layer 3 uncooked noodles and top with meat sauce.
Spread with 1/2 of cottage cheese mixture and 1-1/2 C. meat sauce. Layer 3 more noodles on top of meat sauce. Spread with remaining cottage cheese mixture. Top with remaining 3 uncooked noodles and remaining meat sauce. Pour water around edges.

Freezing and Cooking Directions:

Wrap tightly with freezer paper, foil, or place dish in 2-gallon bag. Label and freeze.
To serve, thaw and bake covered at 375° for 45 minutes. Uncover and bake an additional 15 minutes.
Let stand 10 minutes. Serve with parmesan cheese. To bake from the frozen stage, add 30 minutes to total baking time.
*See our *Zippy Spaghetti Sauce* recipe on page 51.
**If you like your pasta to be firm, decrease the water to 1/2 C. per recipe.

Recipe: Hungarian Stew

Meals:	1	2	3	4	5	6
serves 6-8						

Ingredients:

	1	2	3	4	5	6
lean stew beef	2 lb.	4 lbs.	6 lbs.	8 lbs.	10 lbs.	12 lbs.
olive oil	2 T.	1/4 C.	1/4C.+2T.	1/2 C.	1/2C.+2T.	3/4 C.
salt and pepper to taste						
paprika	1 t.	2 t.	1 T.	1T.+1t.	1T.+2t.	2 T.
garlic, minced	1 t.	2 t.	1 T.	1T.+1t.	1T.+2t.	2 T.
tomato paste	6 oz.	12 oz.	18 oz.	24 oz.	30 oz.	36 oz.
allspice	1/8 t.	1/4 t.	3/8 t.	1/2 t.	1/2t+1/8t	3/4 t.
water	1/2 C.	1 C.	1-1/2C.	2 C.	2-1/2C.	3 C.

On Hand: potatoes, one per adult serving.

Containers: 1-gallon freezer bags or containers suitable for your family

Assembly Directions:
Place the olive oil in a large skillet over medium high heat. Brown the stew beef in the olive oil. Season with salt, pepper, and paprika. Stir well and add garlic, tomato paste, allspice and water. Reduce the heat to simmer and cook covered 2 hours or in crock pot 6-8 hours.

Freezing and Cooking Directions:
Cool, label, and freeze in bags or rigid containers.
To serve, thaw and place stew mixture in a large saucepan. Scrub and cube one potato per person and add to stew mixture. Simmer over medium/low heat. Cook until potatoes are tender, about 15 minutes.
Option: Meat and sauce may be served over mashed, or baked potatoes.

Optional Crock Pot Directions: Place stew and potatoes in a crock pot and simmer 3-4 hours.

Comments:
This is very different from typical stew. It can cook by itself on Assembly Day! Great as leftovers!

Recipe: Master Meat Mix

Meals: serves 4-6	5 C.mix= 1 pan or 60 mtbs.	10 C.= 2 pans or 120 mtbs.	15 C.= 3 pans or 180 mtbs.	20 C.= 4 pans or 240 mtbs.	25 C.= 5 pans or 300 mtbs,	30C.= 6 pans or 360 mtbs.
Ingredients:						
beef, pork, turkey- ground (any 1 or a mixture)	1-1/2 lbs.	3 lbs.	4-1/2 lbs.	6 lbs.	7-1/2 lbs.	9 lbs.
dry oats or cooked brown rice	2/3 C.	1-1/3C.	2 C.	2-2/3C.	3-1/3C.	4 C.
onion, diced	1/2 C.	1 C.	1-1/2C.	2 C.	2-1/2C.	3 C.
salt	1 t.	2 t.	1 T.	1T.+1t.	1T.+ 2t.	2 T.
garlic powder	1/2 t.	1 t.	1-1/2t.	2 t.	2-1/2t.	1 T.
eggs	2	4	6	8	10	12
ketchup or tomato sauce	2/3 C.	1-1/3C.	2 C.	2-2/3C.	3-1/3C.	4 C.

Containers: 1-gallon ziptop bags, 6-cup freezer containers or loaf pans

Assembly Directions:

Mix all ingredients very well with your hands (you may want to wear rubber or disposable gloves) in a large bowl. We have used big, plastic storage containers to do this when making a large quantity. We use this mixture primarily for meatloaf and meatballs. See the *Meatloaf & Meatballs* recipes on page 55.

Recipe: Meatloaf & Meatballs

MEATLOAF

See our Master Meat Mix recipe on page 54 in *Beef Entrees*. 5 cups of this mix will fill a standard meatloaf pan.

Assembly Directions:
Form 5 C. of Master Meat Mix into a loaf in a loaf pan, packing well. Bake at 350° for 1 hour or until no pink shows in the center of the loaf. Cool and chill. Slice meatloaf, if desired.

Freezing and Cooking Directions:
Wrap, label and freeze. On serving day, thaw completely. If it has not been done previously, slice the meatloaf then lay the slices flat on a baking sheet coated with non-stick cooking spray. Brush with one of the optional sauces, if desired. Bake at 350° for 15 minutes or until thoroughly heated.

OR

For every 4 adult servings, place 5 C. of Master Meat Mix in a 1-gallon freezer bag or rigid freezer container. On serving day, thaw completely and press well into loaf shape in a standard loaf pan. Bake as above. (Don't freeze raw meat unless it was fresh, not frozen, when you began.)
Cool loaf for 10 minutes before slicing.

MEATBALLS

Assembly Directions:
Using 5 C. of the Master Meat Mix, form approximately 60 meatballs about the size of large walnuts (or use a small cookie scoop). Place the meatballs on an oiled, (you can use foil if you want to save on clean-up) rimmed baking sheet. Bake at 375° for 20-30 minutes until lightly browned and no longer pink in the center. Cool.

Freezing and Cooking Directions:
Place meatballs in a freezer bag or container. Seal, label and freeze.
To serve, thaw meatballs and bake at 350° for 10-20 minutes until hot.
If using one of the sauces on page 56, thaw meatballs and pour sauce over the meatballs. Bake for 20-30 minutes. Turn the meatballs in the sauce occasionally during the cooking time. These can be served as is or over rice, pasta or potatoes.

Comments:
For some odd reason, meatballs seem to go over better with our kids than a slice of meatloaf even though the meat is exactly the same. Go figure!

Recipe: Seven Sauces for Meatloaf & Meatballs

Each of these sauces is formulated to be used with one meal (5 C.) of our Master Meat Mix. These sauces can be poured over broiled meatballs then baked for 20-30 minutes at 350°. The sauces can be poured over a meatloaf before the last 30 minutes of baking time. Gently turn meatballs in the sauce once or twice during baking to coat them and baste the meatloaf every ten minutes during the last half hour.

If you choose to pre-bake and slice a meatloaf before freezing, we recommend making the sauce on the day it is to be served. The sauce can be brushed over the meatloaf slices during warming and the excess sauce warmed and passed around at the table. For all of these sauces, mix all of the ingredients together, unless otherwise noted.

Salisbury Sauce: 1-1/2 C. *white sauce (or one 10-3/4 oz. can cream of mushroom soup diluted with 1/4 C. water), plus 2 t. Worcestershire sauce.

Barbecue Sauce: 1-1/2 C. of any commercial or homemade barbecue sauce.

Italian Sauce: 2-3 C. of meatless spaghetti sauce can be poured over the baking meatballs and served on spaghetti noodles. 1-1/2 C. sauce can be used on a meatloaf.

Stroganoff Sauce: Pour 1-1/2 C. of *white sauce or one 10-3/4 oz. can cream of mushroom soup over meatballs. Just before serving, gently stir in 8 oz. sour cream.

Teriyaki Sauce:
1/2 C. soy sauce	1/2 C. brown sugar
2 t. vinegar	2 t. cooking oil
1/2 t. ground ginger	1 minced garlic clove

Savory Sauce:
(*Halve this recipe for meatloaf.)

Two 10-3/4 oz. cans tomato soup
2 t. Worcestershire sauce
1-1/4 C. water

Swedish Sauce:
5 T. Worcestershire sauce	4 T. any vinegar
2 T. sugar	1 C. ketchup
1/3 C. water	

COMMENTS:

Any of these sauces will help make the average meatloaf taste just WONDERFUL!
Using different ones could let you serve the same entree once a week but make it taste different each time. Give some a try!
*See white sauce recipes on pages 107 & 108.

Recipe: Swiss Steak

Meals: serves 3-4	1	2	3	4	5	6
Ingredients:						
cubed steaks	1-1/2 lbs.	3 lbs.	4-1/2 lbs.	6 lbs.	7-1/2 lbs.	9 lbs.
flour	1/3 C.	2/3 C.	1 C.	1-1/3C.	1-2/3C.	2 C.
salt	1/2 t.	1 t.	1-1/2t.	2 t.	2-1/2t.	1 T.
celery, diced	2/3 C.	1-1/3C.	2 C.	2-2/3C.	3-1/3C.	4 C.
onion, diced	1/2 C.	1 C.	1-1/2C.	2 C.	2-1/2C.	3 C.
green or red pepper, diced	1 C.	2 C.	3 C.	4 C.	5 C.	6 C.
condensed tomato soup	10 oz.	20 oz.	30 oz.	40 oz.	50 oz.	60 oz.
water	3/4 C.	1-1/2C.	2-1/4C.	3 C.	3-3/4C.	4-1/2C.
Worcestershire sauce	1 T.	2 T.	3 T.	1/4 C.	1/4 C.+1T.	1/4 C.+2T.

Containers: 1-gallon freezer bags

Assembly Directions:

Mix the flour and salt. Coat the meat on both sides with the flour and place in a freezer bag or freezer container and seal. Saute or steam the vegetables until tender. Mix the veggies with the soup, water and Worcestershire sauce. Place the sauce in a quart size freezer bag or container and seal.

Freezing and Cooking Directions:

Label and freeze both containers.
To serve, thaw both bags or containers thoroughly. In a sprayed casserole, place 1/2 C. sauce then alternate layers of meat and sauce, pouring all extra sauce over top of the meat. Cover the pan and bake at 350° for 45-60 minutes or microwave on high for 10 minutes then on medium for 35-40 minutes until the meat is tender and no longer pink in the center. If you choose to microwave, be sure to have it revolve while cooking or turn the pan several times during cooking.
Crock Pot cooking: Layer meat and sauce as above and let it cook 6-8 hours until done.

Comments:

Tara usually microwaves this dish and serves it with rice. The meat is very tender. Nanci baked hers the first time and served it with mashed potatoes. She thought it could be more tender and now does it in the crock pot or microwave.
If your kids hate the veggies, either puree them in the blender or food processor or leave them in large, one-inch chunks that can be easily removed.

Recipe: Shepherd's Pie

Meals:	1	2	3	4	5	6
serves 4-6						

Ingredients:

	1	2	3	4	5	6
butter/margarine	2 T.	1/4 C.	6 T.	1/2 C.	1/2C.+2T.	3/4 C.
onion, chopped	1/2 C.	1 C.	1-1/2 C.	2 C.	2-1/2 C.	3 C.
carrots, chopped	2	4	6	8	10	12
flour	1 T.	2 T.	3 T.	1/4 C.	1/4C.+1T.	1/4C.+2T.
beef broth	2 C. (16oz.)	4 C. (32oz.)	6 C. (48oz.)	8 C. (64oz.)	10 C. (80oz.)	12 C. (96oz.)
tomato sauce	1/2 C.	1 C.	1-1/2 C.	2 C.	2-1/2 C.	3 C.
Worcestershire sauce	1 t.	2 t.	1 T.	1T.+1t.	1T.+2t.	2 T.
oregano	1/4 t.	1/2 t.	3/4 t.	1 t.	1-1/4 t.	1-1/2 t.
salt and pepper to taste						
ground beef or turkey, cooked	2-1/2 C.	5 C.	7-1/2 C.	10 C.	12-1/2 C.	15 C.
*make ahead mashed potatoes	2 C.	4 C.	6 C.	8 C.	10 C.	12 C.

Containers: 8" pie plate(s), 8x8 pan(s) or 1-gallon freezer bags for filling and quart freezer bags for potatoes

Assembly Directions:
Melt butter/margarine in saucepan and fry the onion and carrots until golden brown. Stir in the flour and cook one minute. Gradually stir in beef broth and bring to a boil, stirring constantly. Add the tomato sauce, Worchestershire sauce, oregano and seasonings. Cover the pan. Reduce heat and simmer 15 minutes. Remove from heat and add cooked ground meat. Mix well. Pour into sprayed 8x8 pan, 8" pie plate or freezer bag. If in pan or plate, top with potatoes, wrap with foil or place in a 2-gallon freezer bag. Seal. If in bag, put potatoes in separate bag, label and freeze together.

Freezing and Cooking Directions:
Label and freeze.
To serve, thaw. (If in bags, put filling in pan and spread potatoes on top.) Bake at 400° for 20-30 minutes or until topping is brown and meat is heated through.
To heat from the frozen stage, add 10-15 minutes more baking time.

Comments:
If you like your pie drier, reduce the amount of beef broth.
*See our *Make Ahead Mashed Potatoes* recipe on page 102.

Recipe: Sloppy Joe Casserole

Meals:	1	2	3	4	5	6

serves 4-6

Ingredients:

	1	2	3	4	5	6
salad shell macaroni	8 oz.	16 oz.	24 oz.	32 oz.	40 oz.	48 oz.
sloppy joe mix envelope	1 small	2 small	3 small	4 small	5 small	6 small
ground beef or ground turkey, cooked	1-1/4 C.	2-1/2 C.	3-3/4 C.	5 C.	6-1/4 C.	7-1/2 C.
tomato sauce	8 oz.	16 oz.	24 oz.	32 oz.	40 oz.	48 oz.
tomato paste	6 oz.	12 oz.	18 oz.	24 oz.	30 oz.	36 oz.
water	1 C.	2 C.	3 C.	4 C.	5 C.	6 C.
cottage cheese	16 oz.	32 oz.	48 oz.	64 oz.	80 oz.	96 oz.
cheddar cheese, shredded	1 C. (4 oz.)	2 C. (8 oz.)	3 C. (12 oz.)	4 C. (16 oz.)	5 C. (20 oz.)	6 C. (24 oz.)

Containers: 2-1/2 quart casserole, 8x8 baking dish or 1-gallon freezer bags

Assembly Directions:
Cook macaroni half the recommended time. Drain. Combine seasoning mix with the ground beef or turkey, tomato sauce, tomato paste, and 1 cup water. In sprayed 2-1/2 quart casserole dish or 8x8 baking dish, layer half the macaroni, half the cottage cheese and half the meat sauce; repeat. Top with shredded cheddar cheese. Wrap dish in foil or place in 2-gallon freezer bag. If using freezer bags, freeze the combined pasta and meat sauce and keep the cottage cheese and cheddar cheese on hand to layer the casserole just before baking.

Freezing and Cooking Directions:
Label and freeze.
To serve, thaw (layer in casserole if necessary) and bake uncovered at 350° for 40-50 minutes or until bubbling or place frozen casserole in oven and bake 1 hour 20 minutes.

Comments:
When made with ground turkey or VERY lean ground beef and non-fat cheeses, this recipe only has 1 gram of fat per serving.

Recipe: Marinade for Beef (for steaks, stir fry strips, kabob chunks, etc.)

Meals: serves 4-6	1	2	3	4	5	6
Ingredients:						
beef	2-3 lbs.	4-6 lbs.	6-9 lbs.	8-12 lbs.	10-15 lbs.	12-18lbs.
Marinade:						
lemon juice	1/3 C.	2/3 C.	1 C.	1-1/3C.	1-2/3C.	2 C.
Worcestershire sauce	1/4 C.	1/2 C.	3/4 C.	1 C.	1-1/4C.	1-1/2C.
dry mustard	2 T.	1/4 C.	1/4 C.+2T.	1/2 C.	1/2 C.+2T.	3/4 C.
oil (any kind)	1 C.	2 C.	3 C.	4 C.	5 C.	6 C.
*red wine vinegar	1/2 C.	1 C.	1-1/2C.	2 C.	2-1/2C.	3 C.
*soy sauce (lite &/or reduced salt works fine)	1/2 C.	1 C.	1-1/2C.	2 C.	2-1/2C.	3 C.
black pepper	1 T.	2 T.	3 T.	1/4 C.	1/4C.+1T.	1/4C.+2T.
garlic, minced	2 t.	1T.+1t.	2 T.	2T.+2t.	3T.+1t.	4 T.

Containers: 1-gallon freezer bags or rigid containers suitable for your family

Assembly Directions:
Cut beef into suitable strips or pieces. Place in freezer bags or rigid containers. Combine all marinade ingredients. Pour into freezer bags or containers over meat. (Each meal makes approximately 3 cups.)

Freezing and Cooking Directions:
Label and freeze. Thaw at room temperature or in microwave. Grill or cook beef. Discard marinade.

Comments:
If you like variety, make several of this recipe! Marinated meat is so great to have around. You can decide later what to do with it - the hard part is getting it into the marinade! And if you think meat that has marinated 4 hours tastes good, wait until you try meat that has marinated for 3 weeks!
*We usually buy these items in bulk from a restaurant supply store. It is incredibly cheaper and easier to use than the little bottles.

Recipe: Master Beef Cube Mix and Sauce

Meals:	4 meals or 16 C. (serves 4-5)	8 meals or 32 C. (serves 8-10)	12 meals or 48 C. (serves 12-15)
Ingredients:			
lean stew beef	5 lbs.	10 lbs.	15 lbs.
onion soup mix	1 packet	2 packets	3 packets
bay leaves	2	4	6
*fat free, beef flavored white sauce	6 C.	12 C.	18 C.
mushrooms, minced	1/4 C.	1/2 C.	3/4 C.
celery, minced	1/4 C.	1/2 C.	3/4 C.
water	2 C.	4 C.	6 C.

Containers: 1-gallon freezer bags or rigid containers

Assembly Directions:
Combine all of the above ingredients in a large Dutch oven or covered roasting pan. Stir well. Bake at 300° for about 4 hours or until meat is tender.

Freezing and Cooking Directions:
Cool the mix and pour it into freezer bags or rigid containers. Leave about 1/2" space at top of rigid containers. Label and freeze.
To serve, thaw and serve heated over pasta, rice or potatoes or with *Cowboy Stew* or *Beef Stroganoff*.

Comments:
*See our *Fat Free White Sauce* recipe on page 108.
*See our *Cowboy Stew* recipe on page 62.
*See our *Beef Stroganoff* recipe on page 63.

Recipe: Cowboy Stew

Meals: serves 4-6	1	2	3	4	5	6
Ingredients:						
*beef cube mix	5 C.	10 C.	15 C.	20 C.	25 C.	30 C.
potatoes, diced	5 med.	10 med.	15 med.	20 med.	25 med.	30 med.
carrots, diced	2-1/2 C.	5 C.	7-1/2 C.	10 C.	12-1/2 C.	15 C.
onion, thinly sliced	1 small	2 small	3 small	4 small	5 small	6 small
celery, chopped	1/2 C.	1 C.	1-1/2 C.	2 C.	2-1/2 C.	3 C.
mushrooms	4 oz.	8 oz.	12 oz.	16 oz.	20 oz.	24 oz.
beef or vegetable broth	1/2 C.	1 C.	1-1/2 C.	2 C.	2-1/2 C.	3 C.

Containers: 1-gallon freezer bags or rigid containers suitable for your family

Assembly Directions:

Combine potatoes and carrots in a large saucepan. Add just enough water to cover vegetables. Cook 12-15 minutes until tender. In a small saucepan, cook onion and celery in broth until slightly tender. Use just enough broth to keep the vegetables from sticking. Add mushrooms and saute two more minutes. (In microwave, steam onion and celery in covered container with small amount of water or broth until soft. Add mushrooms and steam an additional two minutes.) Drain liquid from potatoes and carrots. Add vegetables to potatoes and carrots. Stir in beef cube mix.

Freezing and Cooking Directions:

Cool stew and pour it into freezer bags or rigid containers. Leave about 1/2" space at top of rigid containers. Label and freeze.
To serve, thaw beef stew. Simmer about 15-20 minutes until heated through.

Variation: Beef Pot Pie

Put ingredients in a 9x13 baking pan or two pie dishes. Top with pie crust. Flute edges. Cut slits in crust. Wrap in freezer weight foil, or place dish in 2-gallon freezer bag. Freeze.
To serve, thaw and bake at 400° for 30-45 minutes. (May be baked first, then frozen, thawed and reheated.)

Variation: Beef Stew with Biscuit Top

Place the thawed stew in a deep casserole or 9x13 inch baking pan. Prepare one recipe of drop biscuits made from our *Master Baking Mix* on page 122. Drop the biscuit dough by rounded tablespoons onto the beef stew. Bake in a preheated 350° oven until the stew is heated and the biscuit topping is browned, about 30 minutes.

Recipe: Beef Stroganoff

Meals: serves 4-6	**1**	**2**	**3**	**4**	**5**	**6**
Ingredients:						
*beef cube mix	4 C.	8 C.	12 C.	16 C.	20 C.	24 C.
On Hand:						
sour cream	2 C.	4 C.	6 C.	8 C.	10 C.	12 C.

noodles, potatoes, or rice

Containers: 1-gallon freezer bags or rigid containers suitable for your family

Assembly and Cooking Directions:
This entree assembles quickly on the day you will serve it. Thaw the frozen beef cube mix. Over low heat, warm the beef in a saucepan. Just before serving, stir in the sour cream. Serve over hot noodles, cooked rice or potatoes.

Comments:
This tastes much better when combined "fresh" rather than stirring it all up together on cooking day and freezing it.

*See *Master Beef Cube Mix* on page 61.

CHICKEN & TURKEY ENTREES

Parsley Parmesan Chicken

Chicken Enchilada Casserole

Crispy Rice Chicken

Chicken/Turkey Divan

Mediterranean Chicken & Rice

Marinades for Chicken

- Savory Baked Chicken

- Tetrazzini

- Turkey & Noodles

- Chicken Normandy

- Chicken/Turkey Patties

- Chicken Fingers

TIPS FOR POULTRY ENTREES

General Tips For Poultry

✓ We often substitute diced turkey breast for diced chicken. The turkey is so much easier to buy, boil and bone than all those various parts. We think it is the cheapest, too. Turkey meat will have a much firmer texture than chicken.

✓ Don't buy leaking packages. The meat should not be swimming in juices.

✓ Place your poultry on the bottom of your shopping cart in case there are some drips.

✓ Don't let raw meat juices run onto any other foods. Always clean surfaces, mixing bowls, utensils, and hands well after working with raw poultry.

✓ Fresh poultry should not have any noticeable odor.

✓ A large enameled or aluminum water bath canner is very useful. It will hold 2-3 turkey breasts or whole chickens. Placing a trivet or wire rack in the bottom will keep the meat from sticking.

✓ Heavy duty latex gloves or "chicken gloves" as we like to call them, are great for boning and handling hot meat. The meat will come off much quicker when it's hot.

✓ We buy packages of specific parts rather than mixed fryer parts for recipes like *Parsley Parmesan Chicken*. It's hard to find a 3-legged bird if your 3 kids all want a leg. Also, we don't like the waste we have when dealing with necks and backs. You can simmer them for broth, but we usually find that we do not have the time or desire to do this on Assembly Day.

✓ One chicken breast, or two smaller chicken pieces, constitutes an adult serving in our recipes.

✓ Purchase a meat thermometer and learn how to use it! Save the instructions for reviewing.

✓ If you are serving a poultry dish that has been cooked before freezing and merely needs to reheat after thawing, heat it to a temperature of 165° F or until hot and steaming. This is the safest method!

✓ Ground chicken and turkey should be cooked to 165° F to be considered "done". There should be no pink color in the meat or its juices. Whole chickens and turkeys should be cooked to an internal temperature of 180° F. Poultry breasts and roasts should be cooked to 170° F. Thighs and wings should be cooked until the juices run clear with no sign of pink.

✓ If you need boned poultry meat, cook it on the bone whenever possible and then remove the meat from the bones. The bones enhance the flavor of the meat.

✓ Do not freeze stuffed poultry. It is fine to freeze the stuffing separately and fill the poultry with the mixture after thawing if it is to be baked right away.

✓ When figuring how much cooked meat will be yielded from a whole bird, you can usually figure that one cup of meat will come from each pound of bird.

Healthy Tips For Poultry

✓ We always plan for extra diced, cooked poultry to use in nutritious salads and sandwiches. We freeze it in 2-cup portions.

✓ Use fat-free broth whenever possible. Wouldn't you rather consume your fat in hot fudge sundaes than in chicken broth?? To remove the fat from your homemade broth, chill it in the refrigerator until the fat that collects at the top is hard. Use a slotted spatula to lift it out and discard it.

✓ Try our fat free white sauce recipe to replace creamed soups in your own recipes. Bet'cha won't know the difference!

✓ We bake or broil our chicken instead of frying it. Of course, we also remove skin or start with skinless meat. You can really reduce the fat just by following these two rules of thumb.

Recipe: Parsley Parmesan Chicken

Meals:	1	2	3	4	5	6
serves 4-6						

Ingredients:

	1	2	3	4	5	6
Italian salad dressing	1/4 C.	1/2 C.	3/4 C.	1 C.	1-1/4C.	1-1/2C.
fresh fryer parts	2-3 lbs.	5-6 lbs.	8-9 lbs.	11-12 lbs.	14-15 lbs.	17-18 lbs.
grated parmesan cheese	1/2 C.	1 C.	1-1/2C.	2 C.	2-1/2C.	3 C.
dry bread crumbs	1/3 C.	2/3 C.	1 C.	1-1/3C.	1-2/3C.	2 C.
parsley flakes	2 T.	1/4 C.	1/3 C.	1/2 C.	2/3 C.	3/4 C.
paprika	1/2 t.	1 t.	1-1/2t.	2 t.	2-1/2t.	1 T.
salt	1/2 t.	1 t.	1-1/2t.	2 t.	2-1/2t.	1 T.
pepper	1/4 t.	1/2 t.	3/4 t.	1 t.	1-1/4t.	1-1/2t.

Containers: 1-gallon freezer bags for chicken, quart freezer bags for crumbs

Assembly Directions:
To Pre-Bake on Cooking Day: Pour salad dressing in a large bowl. Add the chicken parts to the dressing, coating well. Cover and chill about 4 hours, or overnight. Turn chicken in the dressing occasionally.
Combine parmesan cheese, dry bread crumbs, parsley flakes, paprika, salt and pepper in a shallow bowl. Roll chicken one piece at a time in the crumbs, then place chicken in a greased 9x 13 baking pan or on a cookie sheet. Spoon excess dressing over the chicken. Bake at 350° for 1 hour, or until thickest piece is done.
To Bake on Serving Day: Pour chicken parts and salad dressing into a freezer bag. Combine the parmesan cheese, dry bread crumbs, parsley flakes, paprika, salt and pepper and pour into a quart-sized freezer bag. Attach to the bag of chicken or put both bags into a larger freezer bag.

Freezing and Cooking Directions:
Pre-Baked Chicken:
Remove from oven and cool. Put baked chicken pieces into a freezer bag or rigid freezer container. Label and freeze.
To serve, place chicken in a 9x13 baking dish or pan. Warm in 400° oven for 10 minutes or until warmed through.
Non-Baked Chicken:
Seal, label, and freeze. **To serve,** thaw marinated chicken and crumb mixture. Roll chicken one piece at a time in the crumbs, or shake in a bag, then place chicken in a greased 9x13 pan or on a cookie sheet. Spoon excess dressing over the chicken. Bake at 350° for 1 hour or until thickest piece is done.

Comments:
Having the chicken already baked can really come in handy if you don't have an hour before dinnertime. We especially recommend pre-baking dark meat poultry because it stays moist during re-heating. Diet dressing works fine. Foil-lined cookie sheets help speed the clean up if you bake lots of chicken on Assembly Day.

Recipe: Chicken Enchilada Casserole

Meals:	1	2	3	4	5	6

serves 6-8 (1 recipe makes 2-9" rounds or 1 9x13 pan)

Ingredients:

Ingredient	1	2	3	4	5	6
10" flour tortillas	4	8	12	16	20	24
chicken; cooked, diced	3 C.	6 C.	9 C.	12 C.	15 C.	18 C.
*white sauce, chicken flavored OR	6 C.	12 C.	18 C.	24 C.	30 C.	36 C.
cream of chicken soup, canned/undiluted	42 oz.	84 oz.	126 oz.	168 oz.	210 oz.	252 oz.
cheddar cheese, shredded	1 C.	2 C.	3 C.	4 C.	5 C.	6 C.

Containers: 2-9" round pans/dishes, 9x13 pan, or freezer bags

Assembly Directions:
Place 1 cup of white sauce in the bottom of 9" round dishes or 9x13 pan and spread to moisten the bottom layer. Tear or cut tortillas into strips for 9x13 or square pans. For round pans, tortillas may be left whole. Place 1/2 the tortilla strips or 1 whole tortilla into the bottom of the pan. Layer 1/2 the chicken on the tortillas. Pour 1/2 the sauce over the chicken. Repeat the layers, ending with sauce. Sprinkle cheese over top.

Freezing and Cooking Directions:
Wrap tightly with freezer paper, foil, or place in 2-gallon ziptop bag. (An 8" or 9" pie pan will fit in a 1-gallon freezer bag.)
To serve, thaw and bake at 350° for 20-30 minutes. If this recipe is frozen in a metal or rigid plastic container, it can be popped out frozen and placed in a glass or microwave safe pan and thawed in the microwave 20 minutes, then baked in the oven. If you do this, you may want to put the cheese in a separate small freezer bag (for obvious reasons!).
To bake from the frozen stage, add 10-15 minutes extra baking time.

Comments:
We don't recommend pre-cooking this on Assembly Day since it bakes so quickly.
Options: *Enchiladas:*1/3 *of the white sauce may be stirred into the chicken and used as a filling to roll enchiladas. Spread 1/4-1/3 C. chicken/sauce mixture in each tortilla and roll up. Place each roll seam side down in a spray-treated or greased pan. Top with remaining sauce, then sprinkle on the cheese. Bake as directed above.*
***OR,** freeze the chicken and sauce together. Thaw, warm and serve over potatoes, rice, biscuits, or pasta. Yummy!*
***OR,** stir 2 T. of taco seasoning mix per recipe into the white sauce for more south-of-the-border flavor.*
**See white sauce recipes on pages 107 & 108.*

Recipe: Crispy Rice Chicken

Meals:	1	2	3	4	5	6
serves 4-6						

Ingredients:

	1	2	3	4	5	6
fresh fryer parts	2-3 lbs.	5-6 lbs.	8-9 lbs.	11-12 lbs.	14-15 lbs.	17-18 lbs.
eggs, beaten	1	2	3	4	5	6
water	1/2 C.	1 C.	1-1/2C.	2 C.	2-1/2C.	3 C.
crispy rice cereal, coarsely crushed	1-1/2C.	3 C.	4-1/2C.	6 C.	7-1/2C.	9 C.
garlic powder	1/2 t.	1 t.	1-1/2t.	2 t.	2-1/2t.	1 T.
salt	1/2 t.	1 t.	1-1/2t.	2 t.	2-1/2t.	1 T.
pepper	1/4 t.	1/2 t.	3/4 t.	1 t.	1-1/4t.	1-1/2t.

Containers: 1-gallon freezer bags or rigid containers

Assembly Directions:
To Pre-Bake on Cooking Day:
Rinse and pat dry fryer parts. Beat the egg and water together in a shallow bowl. Place cereal crumbs in another shallow bowl and mix in the garlic powder, salt, and pepper. Dip the fryer parts in the egg mixture, then roll in the crumb mixture to coat all sides. Place each piece in a spray treated or foil-lined 9x13 baking pan, or shallow baking dish. Pre-bake 45 minutes at 350° or until juices run clear. Cool.
To Bake on Serving Day:
Prepare chicken and coat as above. Do not bake.

Freezing and Cooking Directions:
Pre-Baked Chicken:
Remove from oven and cool. Put baked chicken pieces into a freezer bag or rigid container. Label and freeze.
To serve, place chicken in a 9x13 baking dish or pan. Finish baking at 350° for 20-30 minutes until hot and browned. .
Non-Baked Chicken:
Place coated chicken in gallon freezer bags or rigid containers. Label and freeze. If using freezer bags, you may want to "open freeze" the chicken first. Place chicken on a baking sheet and place it in the freezer, uncovered, until firm. Remove and put into freezer bags. This will help keep the coating on the chicken and will keep the pieces from freezing to each other.
To serve, thaw coated chicken pieces and place in spray treated or foil-lined 9x13 pan or shallow baking dish. Bake uncovered at 350° for 1 hour.
Comments:
Having the chicken already baked can really come in handy if you don't have an hour before dinnertime. Foil-lined cookie sheets help speed the clean up if you bake lots of chicken on Assembly Day.

Recipe: Chicken/Turkey Divan

Meals:	1	2	3	4	5	6

serves 6 (1 recipe makes 2-9" rounds or 1-9x13 pan)

Ingredients:

	1	2	3	4	5	6
cooked rice, white or brown	3 C.	6 C.	9 C.	12 C.	15 C.	18 C.
fresh chicken breast fillets	8	16	24	32	40	48
OR						
cooked, diced chicken or turkey	6 C.	12 C.	18 C.	24 C.	30 C.	36 C.
mayonnaise	1 C.	2 C.	3 C.	4 C.	5 C.	6 C.
*white sauce, chicken flavored	3 C.	6 C.	9 C.	12 C.	15 C.	18 C.
OR						
cream soup, canned (chicken, mushroom, or broccoli/undiluted)	21 oz.	42 oz.	63 oz.	84 oz.	105 oz.	126 oz.
lemon juice	2 T.	1/4 C.	1/3 C.	1/2 C.	2/3 C.	3/4 C.
broccoli, frozen (chopped or spears)	20 oz.	40 oz.	60 oz.	80 oz.	100 oz.	120 oz.
cheddar cheese, grated	1 C.	2 C.	3 C.	4 C.	5 C.	6 C.

Containers: 2-9" round pans/dishes or 9x13 pan or freezer bags

Assembly Directions:
Cook and dice chicken or turkey if using diced poultry. Cook rice 3/4 the recommended time. Cook broccoli according to package directions. Set aside. Mix lemon juice and mayonnaise, then add chicken flavored white sauce or soup. Spread rice in container. Layer on broccoli, then half the sauce, then the chicken, then remaining sauce. Top with grated cheese.

Freezing and Cooking Directions:
Wrap tightly with freezer paper, foil, or 2-gallon freezer bag. Seal, label and freeze.
To serve, thaw and bake at 350° for 30 minutes or until chicken is tender and easily pierced with a fork.

Comments:
We don't recommend pre-cooking this on Assembly Day since it bakes so quickly.
If using chopped poultry, you can mix all the ingredients together except the cheese. Freeze rice, chicken, broccoli, and sauce in one bag and cheese topping in another. When ready to serve, thaw then pour into casserole. Top with cheese and bake.
*See white sauce recipes on pages 107 & 108.

Recipe: Mediterranean Chicken & Rice

Meals: serves 4-6	1	2	3	4	5	6
Ingredients:						
boneless chicken breasts or fryer parts (fresh or frozen)	7	14	21	28	35	42
olive oil	1/4 C.	1/2 C.	3/4 C.	1 C.	1-1/4C.	1-1/2C.
garlic, minced	1 t.	2 t.	1 T.	1T. + 1t.	1T. + 2t.	2 T.
onion, chopped	1/2 C.	1 C.	1-1/2C.	2 C.	2-1/2C.	3 C.
gr. pepper, chopped (optional)	1-1/2C.	3 C.	4-1/2C.	6 C.	7-1/2C.	9 C.
red pepper (optional)	1/4 t.	1/2 t.	3/4 t.	1 t.	1-1/4t.	1-1/2t.
tomatoes, crushed	8 oz.	16 oz.	24 oz.	32 oz.	40 oz.	48 oz.
chicken broth	3-1/2C.	7 C.	10-1/2C.	14 C.	17-1/2C.	21 C.
On Hand:						
quick rice, uncooked	1-1/2C.	3 C.	4-1/2C.	6 C.	7-1/2C.	9 C.

Containers: 1-gallon freezer bags or rigid containers.

Assembly Directions:
Brown chicken breast in olive oil. Add garlic, onions, and pepper (optional). Add tomatoes. Simmer till fork tender or till juices run clear. Cool. Place chicken mixture in freezer bags or containers. Pour broth over top.
Seal, label and freeze.

Optional: Measure out rice and put in freezer bag. Attach to chicken and sauce.

Freezing and Cooking Directions:
Freeze chicken and sauce in rigid containers or ziptop bags. Label.
To serve, thaw chicken and sauce. Place the uncooked rice in the bottom of a baking pan. Arrange chicken pieces over rice. Pour sauce over all. Bake uncovered at 350° for 45-50 minutes. Do not stir casserole.

Recipe: Debbie's (Tara's Sister in law) Chicken Marinade

Meals: serves 4-6	**1**	**2**	**3**	**4**	**5**	**6**
Ingredients:						
boneless, skinless chicken breasts	7 pcs.	14 pcs.	21 pcs.	28 pcs.	35 pcs.	42 pcs.
Marinade:						
salt	2 t.	1T.+1t.	2 T.	2T.+2t.	3T.+1t.	4 T.
*Worchestershire sauce	1/4 C.	1/2 C.	3/4 C.	1 C.	1-1/4C.	1-1/2C.
dry mustard	2 T.	1/4 C.	1/4C.+2T.	1/2 C.	1/2C.+2T.	3/4 C.
oil (any kind)	1 C.	2 C.	3 C.	4 C.	5 C.	6 C.
*red wine vinegar	1/2 C.	1 C.	1-1/2C.	2 C.	2-1/2C.	3 C.
*soy sauce (lite &/or reduced salt works fine)	3/4 C.	1-1/2C.	2-1/4C.	3 C.	3-3/4C.	4-1/2C.
pepper	1 t.	2 t.	1 T.	1T.+1t.	1T.+2t.	2 T.
garlic, minced	1 t.	2 t.	1 T.	1T.+1t.	1T.+2t.	2 T.
parsley flakes	1-1/2t.	1 T.	1T.+1-1/2t.	2 T.	2T.+1-1/2t.	3 T.

Containers: 1-gallon freezer bags or rigid containers suitable for your family

Assembly Directions:
Combine all marinade ingredients. Place chicken pieces in 1-gallon freezer bag or rigid container. Pour marinade over the meat. (Each recipe makes approximately 3 cups.)

Freezing and Cooking Directions:
Label and freeze.
To serve, thaw. Grill or cook chicken until the meat is no longer pink inside and the juices run clear. Discard marinade.
For Chicken Strips: Cut chicken breasts into strips and marinade to use for stir fry, fajitas, or hot off the grill!

Comments:
Great to have on hand for grilling season or anytime! (Nanci makes her husband clean snow off the grill to serve this in the winter!) Also a wonderful company meal. Just pull out two or three bags instead of one!
*We usually buy these items in bulk from a restaurant supply store. It is incredibly cheaper and easier to use than the little bottles.

Recipe: Teriyaki Chicken Marinade for Stir Fry

Meals:	1	2	3	4	5	6
serves 4						

Ingredients:

	1	2	3	4	5	6
boneless, skinless chicken breasts (sliced into 1/4" thin strips)	1-1/2 lbs.	3 lbs.	4-1/2 lbs.	6 lbs.	7-1/2 lbs.	9 lbs.

Marinade:

	1	2	3	4	5	6
ginger, powdered	1/4 t.	1/2 t.	3/4 t.	1 t.	1-1/4 t.	1-1/2 t.
dry mustard	2 t.	1T.+1t.	2T.	2T.+2t.	3T.+1t.	1/4 C.
oil (any kind)	1/4 C.	1/2 C.	3/4 C.	1 C.	1-1/4 C.	1-1/2 C.
*soy sauce (lite &/or reduced salt works fine)	1/2 C.	1 C.	1-1/2C.	2 C.	2-1/2C.	3 C.
garlic, minced	1 t.	2 t.	1 T.	1T.+1t.	1T.+2t.	2 T.
molasses	2 T.	1/4 C.	1/4C.+2T.	1/2 C.	1/2C.+2T.	3/4 C.

On Hand: 1 to 1-1/2 C. thin sliced, raw vegetables per adult (zucchini, onions, carrots, spinach, bok choy, mushrooms, celery, peppers, bamboo shoots, etc., in any combination) and rice or pasta
Containers: 1-gallon freezer bags or rigid containers

Assembly Directions:

Combine all marinade ingredients. Place chicken strips in freezer bag or rigid container. Pour marinade over the meat. (Each meal makes approximately 1 C.)

Freezing and Cooking Directions:

Label, seal and freeze.
To serve, thaw the meat and marinade. Heat 2 T. olive oil in a large skillet over medium high heat. A drop of water should sizzle rapidly when dropped into the hot pan. Drain the marinade from the meat and discard. Add the meat strips and cook them rapidly, stirring frequently. Chicken should no longer be pink in the center, but don't overcook. Overcooking will make the meat tough. When cooked, remove the meat from the skillet with a spatula or spoon and keep warm in a covered dish. Add the vegetables to the hot skillet in order of density. The denser vegetables need to cook the longest. Carrots and onions first, then peppers, celery and bok choy about three minutes later, and last add the more tender selections like spinach and zucchini. Stirring constantly, cook the vegetables to the desired amount of doneness. The meat may be stirred back into the pan, or served separately. Serve with hot cooked rice or pasta.

Comments:

Rice or pasta may be cooked ahead of time and frozen in freezer bags for an even faster meal. Just reheat in the microwave!

Recipe: Savory Baked Chicken

Meals: serves 4-6	1	2	3	4	5	6
Ingredients:						
boneless chicken breasts, chopped (fresh) in 1" strips	7	14	21	28	35	42
*white sauce, chicken flavored OR	3 C.	6 C.	9 C.	12 C.	15 C.	18 C.
cream of chicken soup, canned	21 oz.	42 oz.	63 oz.	84 oz.	105 oz.	126 oz.
grated parmesan cheese	1/4 C.	1/2 C.	3/4 C.	1 C.	1-1/4 C.	1-1/2 C.
parsley flakes	1 t.	2 t.	1 T.	1T.+1t.	1T.+2t.	2 T.
oregano	1/4 t.	1/2 t.	3/4 t.	1 t.	1-1/4 t.	1-1/2 t.
basil	1/4 t.	1/2 t.	3/4 t.	1 t.	1-1/4 t.	1-1/2 t.
pepper	1/8 t.	1/4 t.	3/8 t.	1/2 t.	1/2t.+1/8t.	3/4 t.
dry spaghetti	8 oz.	16 oz.	24 oz.	32 oz.	40 oz.	48 oz.
On Hand:						
chicken broth	14 oz.	28 oz.	42 oz.	56 oz.	70 oz.	84 oz.

Containers: 1-gallon and quart freezer bags, 8x8 dish or 2-1/2 quart casserole to serve

Assembly Directions:

Chop fresh, boneless chicken pieces and place in labeled freezer bag. Combine white sauce or soup, parmesan cheese, parsley flakes, oregano, basil and pepper. Put into labeled freezer bag. Spray skillet with cooking spray and heat to medium-high. When pan is hot, pour in pasta, broken in 1" pieces. Watch pasta, turning frequently until golden brown. Remove from heat. When cooled, put into labeled freezer bag. Place all 3 freezer bags together inside a larger labeled freezer bag.

Freezing and Cooking Directions:

Freeze. **To serve,** thaw 3 freezer bags. An hour before serving, preheat oven to 350°. Spray an 8x8 baking dish or a 2-1/2 quart casserole. Place chicken in dish and pour thawed sauce on top. Bake 1 hour or until pieces are tender. 35-40 minutes into baking time, pour broth (on hand) into skillet. Bring to a boil, then add broken pasta. Reduce to simmer and cook until tender. To serve, place chicken pieces on top of pasta on plate. Pass the sauce at the table.

Comments:

This sounds complicated, but it's SO good! Just be sure to plan this for a night when you have an hour before dinner.
*See white sauce recipes on page 107 & 108.

30 DAY GOURMET
CHICKEN ENTREE

Recipe: Chicken or Turkey Tetrazzini

Meals:	1	2	3	4	5	6

serves 4-6

Ingredients:

Ingredient	1	2	3	4	5	6
*white sauce, chicken flavored **OR**	6 C.	12 C.	18 C.	24 C.	30 C.	36 C.
cream soup, canned (chicken or mushroom/undiluted)	42 oz.	84 oz.	126 oz.	168 oz.	210 oz.	252 oz.
lemon juice	2 T.	1/4 C.	1/3 C.	1/2 C.	2/3 C.	3/4 C.
green pepper, diced (opt.)	1/2 C.	1 C.	1-1/2C.	2 C.	2-1/2C.	3 C.
dry spaghetti, broken in 1" pieces	4 C.	8 C.	12 C.	16 C.	20 C.	24 C.
cooked chicken, diced	4 C.	8 C.	12 C.	16 C.	20 C.	24 C.
mushrooms (opt.)	8 oz.	16 oz.	24 oz.	32 oz.	40 oz.	48 oz.
grated parmesan cheese	1 C.	2 C.	3 C.	4 C.	5 C.	6 C.

Containers: 2-1/2 qt. casserole or 1-gallon and quart freezer bags

Assembly Directions:
Combine white sauce or soup and lemon juice. Saute (in a small amount of oil) or steam green pepper and add to sauce. Break spaghetti into 1" pieces and boil in salted water 1/2 the recommended time. Drain spaghetti. Mix spaghetti, chicken or turkey, and mushrooms into sauce.
Optional: Cook spaghetti full recommended time and put in freezer bag. Attach to chicken and sauce. Stir into casserole just before baking.

Freezing and Cooking Directions:
Pour mixture into 2-1/2 qt. casserole and top with grated parmesan cheese. Wrap in freezer paper, foil, or place pan in 2-gallon freezer bag. Label and freeze. OR Pour mixture into 1-gallon freezer bag. Enclose a small freezer bag with 1 C. grated parmesan cheese for each recipe. Label and freeze.
To serve, thaw completely. If in microwave-safe container, heat on medium power 20-30 minutes, or until hot throughout. If in metal pan, bake at 350° for 45-60 minutes or until thoroughly heated. If food is in a freezer bag, thaw, pour contents into an oiled baking dish, sprinkle enclosed cheese on top, and cook as above. Frozen casserole may be baked for 1-1/2 hours at 350°

*See white sauce recipes on pages 107 & 108.

Recipe: Turkey and Noodles

Meals: serves 6-8	1	2	3	4	5	6
Ingredients:						
*turkey or chicken broth	96 oz.	192 oz.	288 oz.	384 oz.	480 oz.	576 oz.
salt	1/2 t.	1 t.	1-1/2t.	2 t.	2-1/2t.	1 T.
onion, diced	1/2 C.	1 C.	1-1/2C.	2 C.	2-1/2C.	3 C.
pepper	1/4 t.	1/2 t.	3/4 t.	1 t.	1-1/4t.	1-1/2t.
frozen egg noodles (or homemade style)	1 lb.	2 lb.	3 lb.	4 lb.	5 lb.	6 lb.
flour	1/4 C.	1/2 C.	3/4 C.	1 C.	1-1/4C.	1-1/2C.
milk	1-1/2C.	3 C.	4-1/2C.	6 C.	7-1/2C.	9 C.
cooked turkey, diced	4 C.	8 C.	12 C.	16 C.	20 C.	24 C.

salt to taste

Containers: 1-gallon freezer bags or rigid containers

Assembly Directions:
In a large pot, heat broth to boiling. Add salt, onion, and pepper. Add frozen noodles and bring again to a boil. Reduce heat to keep from boiling over, but still bubbling freely. Cook 10 minutes. Stir flour and milk together and add to bubbling pot. Cook until juices are somewhat reduced and slightly thickened. Add meat. Salt to taste. Cool.

Freezing and Cooking Directions:
Divide into family-sized portions in freezer bags or rigid containers. Label, seal and freeze.
To serve, thaw and reheat over low heat in saucepan, microwave, or 350° oven 20-30 minutes.

Comments:
Canned or frozen peas, or cooked, sliced carrots may be added with the meat. Add 1 to 1-1/2 C. per recipe.
*For low fat turkey broth, save broth from cooked turkey. Chill it. Remove fat that has risen to the top.
Doing this will also save you lots of money!

Recipe: Chicken Normandy

Meals: serves 4-6	1	2	3	4	5	6
Ingredients:						
chicken breasts or fryer parts	7	14	21	28	35	42
olive or vegetable oil	2 T.	1/4 C.	3/8 C.	1/2 C.	1/2C.+2T.	3/4 C.
onion, diced	1/2 C.	1 C.	1-1/2C.	2 C.	2-1/2C.	3 C.
flour	1/4 C.	1/2 C.	3/4 C.	1 C.	1-1/4C.	1-1/2C.
apple cider or white cooking wine	12 oz.	24 oz.	36 oz.	48 oz.	60 oz.	72 oz.
chicken broth	4 oz.	8 oz.	12 oz.	16 oz.	20 oz.	24 oz.
oregano	1/2 t.	1 t.	1-1/2t.	2 t.	2-1/2t.	1 T.
rosemary	1/4 t.	1/2 t.	3/4 t.	1 t.	1-1/4t.	1-1/2t.
salt & pepper to taste						
cooking apples	4	8	12	16	20	24

Containers: 3-quart casserole, 9x13 baking dish or pan, or 1-gallon freezer bags

Assembly Directions:

To Pre-Bake: Over medium-high heat, heat oil in a frying pan. Add the chicken and fry on both sides until golden brown. Remove and place in 3-quart casserole or 9x13 pan. Lower heat to medium-low. Add onion to the pan and fry until tender. Sprinkle in flour and cook, stirring constantly, until light brown, 1-2 minutes. Gradually stir in apple cider or cooking wine, broth, herbs and bring to a boil. stirring constantly. Cook until thickened. Season to taste with salt and pepper and pour over chicken. Peel and core apples and cut into thick slices. Place apple slices on top of chicken and sauce. Cover casserole. Bake at 350° for 1 hour or until just tender. Cool. Wrap in foil, freezer paper, or place pan in 2-gallon freezer bag. Label and freeze.
To Bake on serving day: Cook chicken and sauce as above. Place browned chicken in 1-gallon freezer bag or rigid container. Pour cooled sauce and sliced apples into another freezer bag. Put both bags inside a larger freezer bag. Label and freeze.

Freezing and Cooking Directions:

Pre-baked chicken: To serve, reheat the frozen casserole (without thawing) covered at 400° for 1 hour or until heated through.
Unbaked chicken: To serve, thaw bags. Place chicken pieces in 3-quart casserole or 9x13 dish/pan. Pour sauce over chicken. Arrange apple slices on top. Bake covered at 350° for 1 hour.

Comments:

This is really yummy! The apples give it a great taste – but if you prefer, omit them.

Recipe: Chicken/Turkey Patties

Meals:	12 patties	24 patties	36 patties	48 patties	60 patties	72 patties
Ingredients:						
*cooked chicken or turkey, finely minced	4 C.	8 C.	12 C.	16 C.	20 C.	24 C.
eggs, lightly beaten	4	8	12	16	20	24
grated parmesan cheese	1 C.	2 C.	3 C.	4 C.	5 C.	6 C.
fine, dry bread crumbs	1/2 C.	1 C.	1-1/2C.	2 C.	2-1/2C.	3 C.
olive or canola oil	2 T.	1/4 C.	6 T.	1/2 C.	1/2C.+2T.	3/4 C.

On Hand: For Parmigiana; spaghetti sauce and shredded mozzarella cheese

Containers: freezer bags or rigid containers

Assembly Directions:
Combine all the ingredients well. Use your hands to make 12 round or oval patties, 1/2" thick. Heat the oil in a skillet. Saute the patties on each side until browned. (This may also be done under the broiler.) Cool thoroughly.

Freezing and Cooking Directions:
Freeze in freezer bags or rigid containers. Place waxed paper or plastic wrap between the slices.
To serve, thaw and reheat in a skillet, microwave, or oven at 350° for about 10 minutes.
For Parmigiana: On the day you will eat it, thaw the patties. In a flat bottomed baking dish, place 1/2 C. spaghetti sauce. Spread this evenly over the bottom of the dish. Place the patties in the pan, one at a time, topping each patty with 2 T. or so of spaghetti sauce, and 2 T. or so mozzarella cheese. The patties should overlap each other slightly. Pour as much additional sauce as you wish over the patties evenly. Top with additional shredded mozzarella cheese if you like. Heat in a 350° oven for 30-40 minutes, or until heated through.

Comments:
This recipe has become a tradition for both of our families. It is delicious, versatile and VERY easy. These are good as sandwiches or served with gravy and potatoes or ketchup and fries, and even as Parmigiana.

*The cooked chicken is easily minced in a food processor. A blender and food grinder would do fine, but to do it by hand would be very tedious.

Recipe: Baked Chicken Fingers/Nuggets

Fingers:	**36**	**72**	**108**	**144**	**180**	**216**
serves 4-6						

Ingredients:

	36	72	108	144	180	216
boneless, skinless chicken breasts (cut into lengthwise strips or nuggets)	2 lbs.	4 lbs.	6 lbs.	8 lbs.	10 lbs.	12 lbs.

Sauce #1:

	36	72	108	144	180	216
mayonnaise	1/4 C.	1/2 C.	3/4 C.	1 C.	1-1/4 C.	1-1/2 C.
milk	1/4 C.	1/2 C.	3/4 C.	1 C.	1-1/4 C.	1-1/2 C.
dry mustard	2 t.	1T.+1t.	2T.	2T.+2t.	3T.+1t.	1/4 C.
onion powder	1 t.	2 t.	1 T.	1T.+1t.	1T.+2t.	2 T.

OR

Sauce #2:

	36	72	108	144	180	216
milk	1/4 C.	1/2 C.	3/4 C.	1 C.	1-1/4 C.	1-1/2 C.
ranch dressing;bottled	1/4 C.	1/2 C.	3/4 C.	1 C.	1-1/4 C.	1-1/2 C.

Coating:

	36	72	108	144	180	216
bread crumbs or cracker meal	1 C.	2 C.	3 C.	4 C.	5 C.	6 C.
paprika	1/2 t.	1 t.	1-1/2 t.	2 t.	2-1/2 t.	1 T.

Containers: 1-gallon freezer bags or rigid containers

Assembly Directions:

Choose one sauce, then mix all of its ingredients together well with a wire whisk, mixer, or spoon. Cut chicken breasts into lengthwise strips or nuggets. Place all of the chicken pieces in the sauce and stir well to coat. Place coating in a plastic bag, bowl or other container with a lid. Place about one pound of chicken (or 1/2 a single recipe), in the crumb mixture. Seal container and shake well to coat pieces with crumbs. Place chicken on spray-treated or greased baking sheets and bake at 375° for 15-20 minutes, turning once. Remove from oven and cool on baking sheets.

Freezing and Cooking Directions:

When cool, place trays of fingers or nuggets in freezer and freeze until firm. Place frozen fingers or nuggets in freezer bags or rigid containers.
To serve, place frozen fingers or nuggets on a baking sheet and reheat at 400° for 5-10 minutes until sizzling and hot.

Comments:

These have so many great uses! Our kids love them. To make them lower in fat, use skim milk, fat free mayonnaise, and diet ranch dressing. You'll never miss the fat!

PORK & FISH ENTREES

- Ham Loaf/Ham Balls
- Ham Sauces
- Ham & Potato Casserole
- Pork Barbecue
- Marinade for Pork

- Sausage Rice Bake
- Mexican Pork Chops
- Breaded Fish Fillets
- West Country Cod
- Citrus Marinade for Fish

TIPS FOR PORK & FISH ENTREES

General Tips For Pork and Fish

✓ Most fresh fish should not have a strong "fishy" odor and the packages should not be leaking.

✓ Fresh fish steaks and fillets should be firm. When you lightly press on the fish with your finger, the flesh should spring back into shape.

✓ When choosing fish for the grill, the firmer the better. Salmon, swordfish, tuna and halibut are perfect for grilling. Steaks that are one to two inches thick work best.

✓ As a general rule, the lighter the color, the lighter the flavor. Sole, Pacific and Atlantic halibut, cod, flounder, grouper, sea or fresh water bass, haddock, orange roughy, and trout are some of the milder tasting fish varieties. Ling cod, snapper, whiting, perch, rockfish, bluefish, catfish, and salmon are considered to be in the moderate flavored range. Swordfish, mackerel, shad and tuna are some of the stronger flavored fish varieties.

✓ Generally, ten minutes of cooking time per inch of thickness is a good rule. If a fish variety is translucent (sort of clear) to begin with, it is done as soon as it is opaque (not clear). When you are sauteeing fish, the pan is too hot if you can smell the fish.

✓ 1/4 lb. of raw fish is an adult serving.

✓ 1/4 C. of cooked ground pork (as in sausage), is an adult serving.

✓ Cured pork products like ham and bacon should only be frozen for a month, or they will develop a strong flavor.

✓ You can grind your own ham in a food processor or ask your butcher to do it. When doing it yourself, cut the ham into 2" cubes and use the chopping blade. Pulse the blade until it is evenly ground. Experiment with textures.

✓ Purchase a meat thermometer and learn how to use it. Save the directions for review later.

✓ Pork roasts, steaks, and chops are considered medium done if the internal temperature reaches 160° F. Well done roasts, steaks and chops will have a temperature of 170° F.

✓ When choosing ribs for barbecuing, country style ribs will have quite a bit more meat on them.

Healthy Tips For Pork and Fish

✓ Broil, bake, or grill fish instead of frying it in fat.

✓ Sole, Pacific halibut, cod, flounder, grouper, sea bass, haddock, orange roughy, ling cod, red snapper, whiting, perch, pike, and rockfish all have less than 11 grams of fat per pound.

✓ The higher fat fish varieties are pompano, mackerel, sablefish, and shad. These varieties all have more than 23 grams of fat per pound. Most other varieties range between 11 and 23 grams of fat per pound.

✓ To cut down on your red meat intake, ask the butcher to mix in an equal quantity of ground turkey with your ground pork.

✓ You can automatically cut out many fat grams by trimming all the visible fat from the outsides of steaks and chops.

✓ Boneless pork loin chops are a lower fat chop compared to other cuts, but be careful not to over-cook them or they will be very dry and chewy!

Recipe: Ham Loaf/ Ham Balls

Meals:	1	2	3	4	5	6
serves 4-6

Ingredients:

	1	2	3	4	5	6
ground ham, cooked	1-1/2 lbs.	3 lbs.	4-1/2 lbs.	6 lbs.	7-1/2 lbs.	9 lbs.
lean ground beef, uncooked	3/4 lbs.	1-1/2 lbs.	2-1/4 lbs.	3 lbs.	3-3/4 lbs.	4-1/2 lbs.
eggs	2	4	6	8	10	12
prepared mustard	2 t.	1T.+1t.	2 T.	2T.+2t.	3T.+1t.	1/4 C.
salt	1/2 t.	1 t.	1-1/2t.	2 t.	2-1/2t.	1 T.
milk	1 C.	2 C.	3 C.	4 C.	5 C.	6 C.
fine soda cracker crumbs	3/4 C.	1-1/2C.	2-1/4C.	3 C.	3-3/4C.	4-1/2C.

Containers: 1-gallon freezer bags or loaf pans

Assembly Directions:
Combine all the ingredients in a large bowl. Mix very well with your hands. (If you don't like the thought of that, use rubber or disposable gloves.)

Freezing and Cooking Directions:
Place the mixture in 1-gallon freezer bags or in 9x5x3 loaf pans, well wrapped. Label and freeze. Freezing guidelines recommend that you do not freeze ham for longer than 1 month.
To serve, thaw. Remove from freezer bag (if necessary) and shape into loaf into an oiled 9x5x3 pan. Cover pan with foil. Bake at 325° for a total of 75 minutes. While the loaf is baking, prepare one of the sauces on page 84. After 30 minutes of baking time, add the sauce. Baste every 10-15 minutes till done.

Ham Balls: For ham balls, just shape the mixture into walnut sized balls. We use a cookie scoop for quicker and more uniform ham balls. Bake 45 minutes at 350°, adding sauce after 15 minutes.

Comments:
As with most of our recipes, you may bake the entree on Assembly Day, cool and freeze or you may freeze it uncooked and do it later. Your choice generally depends on how much dinner prep time you have each day.

Recipe: Nine Sauces for Ham Loaf & Ham Balls

For each of these sauces, mix all the ingredients together. Add to the ham loaf after 30 minutes of baking time. Baste the meat with the sauce every 10 minutes after that. Add to the ham balls after 15 minutes of baking time. Pass any extra sauce with the meat at the table. Both the loaf and the ham balls may be fully cooked with the sauce and then frozen together for a quicker warm up time before serving.

Ham Sauce 1:

1-3/4 C. brown sugar
1 T. water

2 t. prepared mustard
1 T. vinegar

Ham Sauce 2:

1 C. brown sugar
2 t. dry mustard

1/4 C. maple syrup or honey
1 small can of crushed
pineapple, drained

Ham Sauce 3:

16 oz. can whole cranberry sauce
1 T. prepared mustard
1-1/2 t. vinegar

Ham Sauce 4:

1/2 C. raisins
1 t. dry mustard
2 T. molasses
1/4 C. water

3 T. flour
3 T. vinegar
1 T. beef bouillon granules
(3 cubes, crushed)

Ham Sauce 5:

1 C. currant jelly

2 T. prepared mustard

Ham Sauce 6:

1/4 C. apricot jam
2 t. dijon-type mustard

2 t. vinegar

Ham Sauce 7:

1/2 C. water (or pineapple juice)
1 T. cornstarch
1 T. soy sauce
1/4 C. vinegar

1 T. ketchup
1/4 C. sugar

Ham Sauce 8:

3/4 to 1 C. of any barbecue sauce

Ham Sauce 9:

3/4 C. pineapple juice
1/3 C. soy sauce

1 T. cornstarch
3 T. honey

Recipe: Ham & Potato Casserole/Scalloped Potatoes

Meals: serves 6-8	1	2	3	4	5	6
Ingredients:						
hash browns; frozen, cubed	2 lbs.	4 lbs.	6 lbs.	8 lbs.	10 lbs.	12 lbs.
*white sauce	1-1/2C.	3 C.	4-1/2C.	6 C.	7-1/2C.	9 C.
butter/margarine, melted	2 T.	4 T.	6 T.	8 T.	10 T.	12 T.
sour cream	16 oz.	32 oz.	48 oz.	64 oz.	80 oz.	96 oz.
cooked ham, cubed	2 C.	4 C.	6 C.	8 C.	10 C.	12 C.
pepper	1/2 t.	1 t.	1-1/2t.	2 t.	2-1/2t.	1 T.
green onion, chopped	1/3 C.	2/3 C.	1 C.	1-1/3C.	1-2/3C.	2 C.
cheddar cheese, shredded	1 C. (4 oz.)	2 C. (8 oz.)	3 C. (12 oz.)	4 C. (16 oz.)	5 C. (20 oz.)	6 C. (24 oz.)
corn flakes, crushed	2 C.	4 C.	6 C.	8 C.	10 C.	12 C.
margarine, melted	1/4 C.	1/2 C.	3/4 C.	1 C.	1-1/4C.	1-1/2C.

Containers: 1-gallon freezer bags, rigid freezer containers or 9x13 pans

Assembly Directions:
Combine first 8 ingredients and mix well. Place this mixture in a 9x13 pan, two smaller pans, 1-gallon freezer bags or rigid freezer containers. Combine corn flake crumbs and margarine/butter. Sprinkle these over pans or place in separate freezer bags.
For Scalloped Potatoes: Omit ham and assemble the same.

Freezing and Cooking Directions:
Cover casserole tightly with foil, freezer wrap or place pan in 2-gallon freezer bag. Seal bags well, squeezing out excess air. Label and freeze.
To serve, thaw completely. If necessary, sprinkle with cornflake topping. Bake at 350° for 1 hour. Frozen casserole may be baked for 1-1/2 hours at 350°.

Comments:
*Be sure to freeze the bag of crumbs WITH the casserole or you will lose them! And yes, it is best to do the crumb topping now. In our experience, those corn flakes will never be there the day you need them!
*Mixing this in a LARGE pot or plastic tub with your hands is the quickest but you may get frostbite! Wear thick rubber gloves. They work great!
*For a lower fat meal, use our fat free white sauce along with lower or fat free sour cream and cheese.

*See white sauce recipes on pages 107 & 108.

Recipe: Pork Barbecue

Meals:	1	2	3	4	5	6
serves 4-6						

Ingredients:

	1	2	3	4	5	6
onion, chopped	1/2 C.	1 C.	1-1/2C.	2 C.	2-1/2C.	3 C.
celery, chopped	1/4 C.	1/2 C.	3/4 C.	1 C.	1-1/4C.	1-1/2C.
ketchup	1/2 C.	1 C.	1-1/2C.	2 C.	2-1/2C.	3 C.
water	1/3 C.	2/3 C.	1 C.	1-1/3C.	1-2/3C.	2 C.
lemon juice	2 T.	1/4 C.	1/4C.+2T.	1/2 C.	1/2C.+2T.	3/4 C.
brown sugar or molasses	1 T.	2 T.	3 T.	1/4 C.	1/4C.+1T.	1/4C.+2T.
Worcestershire sauce	1 T.	2 T.	3 T.	1/4 C.	1/4C.+1T.	1/4C.+2T.
vinegar	1 T.	2 T.	3 T.	1/4 C.	1/4C.+1T.	1/4C.+2T.
prepared mustard	1 T.	2 T.	3 T.	1/4 C.	1/4C.+1T.	1/4C.+2T.
salt and pepper to taste						
pork roast	1-1/2 lb.	3 lb.	4-1/2 lb.	6 lb.	7-1/2 lb.	9 lb.

On Hand: hoagie rolls or sandwich buns

Containers: 1-gallon freezer bags or rigid containers

Assembly Directions:
In crock pot, stir all ingredients together except the meat. Set the meat on top of the sauce and simmer until meat is easily shredded with a fork. Simmer 6-8 hours or overnight. Shred the meat while it is warm. Stir in the sauce well. The barbequed pork is now ready to eat, or cool for freezing.

Freezing and Cooking Directions:
When the meat is cool, portion it into freezer bags or rigid containers. Seal, label, and freeze.
To serve, thaw. Heat the meat in the microwave, in a saucepan on low, or in the oven at 350° until hot (15-20 minutes per recipe).

Options:*Add a few drops of liquid smoke for a smoky flavor.
*Diced bell peppers may be added to the sauce ingredients: 1/2-1 C. pepper per recipe.

Recipe: Marinade for Pork

Meals:	1	2	3	4	5	6
serves 4-6						

Ingredients:

	1	2	3	4	5	6
pork chops	6-8	12-16	18-24	24-32	30-40	36-48

Marinade:

	1	2	3	4	5	6
pineapple juice	16 oz.	32 oz.	48 oz.	64 oz.	80 oz.	96 oz.
*soy sauce (lite &/or reduced salt works fine)	1/2 C.	1 C.	1-1/2C.	2 C.	2-1/2C.	3 C.
ginger, ground	1 t.	2 t.	1 T.	1T.+ 1t.	1T.+ 2t.	2 T.
garlic, minced	1/2 t.	1 t.	1-1/2t.	2 t.	2-1/2t.	1 T.
italian dressing (diet is fine)	1/3 C.	2/3 C.	1 C.	1-1/3C.	1-2/3C.	2 C.

Containers: 1-gallon freezer bags or rigid containers

Assembly Directions:
Combine all marinade ingredients. Place meat in freezer bags or containers. Pour marinade over meat. (Each meal makes approximately 3 cups.)

Freezing and Cooking Directions:
Label, seal and freeze.
To serve, thaw. Grill, broil, or pan fry pork chops until browned on both sides and no longer pink in the center. Discard marinade.

Comments:
We usually buy our soy sauce at a restaurant supply store where it is MUCH cheaper!

Recipe: Sausage Rice Bake

Meals:	1	2	3	4	5	6
serves 4-6						

Ingredients:

	1	2	3	4	5	6
onion, minced	1/2 C.	1 C.	1-1/2C.	2 C.	2-1/2C.	3 C.
bulk pork turkey sausage	1/2 lb.	1 lb.	1-1/2 lb.	2 lb.	2-1/2 lb.	3 lb.
olive oil	3 T.	6 T.	1/2C.+ 1T.	3/4 C.	3/4C.+ 3T.	1C.+2T.
frozen peas (or any cooked/blanched veggie)	8 oz.	16 oz.	24 oz.	32 oz.	40 oz.	48 oz.
sliced mushrooms	4-1/2 oz.	9 oz.	13-1/2 oz.	18 oz.	22-1/2 oz.	27 oz.
beef broth	3/4 C.	1-1/2C.	2-1/4C.	3 C.	3-3/4C.	4-1/2C.
instant brown rice, uncooked	2 C.	4 C.	6 C.	8 C.	10 C.	12 C.
beef broth	1-1/2C.	3 C.	4-1/2C.	6 C.	7-1/2C.	9 C.

On Hand: **parmesan cheese, canned artichoke hearts (optional) and sliced olives (optional)**

Containers: 1-gallon freezer bags or 8x8 casserole

Assembly Directions:
Saute minced onions and pork or turkey sausage in olive oil until browned. Add frozen peas (or other cooked vegetable), mushrooms and beef broth. Simmer 10 minutes. Stir in uncooked rice and broth. Toss lightly and cool. (It will absorb the broth.)

Freezing and Cooking Directions:
Divide into suitable portions. Seal, label and freeze.
To serve, thaw freezer bag or casserole. Stir in 1/2 C. water for each meal. If in bag, turn into sprayed 8x8 casserole. Sprinkle top with grated parmesan cheese. Bake at 375° for 20-30 minutes until rice is done.

Comments:
Using lean turkey sausage will keep this recipe the lowest in fat but any kind of sausage will work. Watch the "hotness" of the meat.
Options: Marinated artichokes or sliced black or green olives are very good stirred into this dish. Keep them on hand and stir in just before topping with parmesan cheese.

Recipe: Mexican Pork Chops

Meals: serves 4	1	2	3	4	5	6
Ingredients:						
pork chops	6	12	18	24	30	36
vegetable oil	2 T.	1/4 C.	1/4C.+2T.	1/2 C.	1/2C.+ 2T.	3/4 C.
water	1-1/2C.	3 C.	4-1/2C.	6 C.	7-1/2C.	9 C.
long grain rice, uncooked	3/4 C.	1-1/2C.	2-1/4C.	3 C.	3-3/4C.	4-1/2C.
tomato sauce	8 oz.	16 oz.	24 oz.	32 oz.	40 oz.	48 oz.
taco seasoning mix	2 T.	1 packet	6 T.	2 packets	1/2C.+2T.	3 packets
green pepper, chopped	1 med.	2 med.	3 med.	4 med.	5 med.	6 med.
cheddar cheese, shredded	1 C. (4 oz.)	2 C. (8 oz.)	3 C. (12 oz.)	4 C. (16 oz.)	5 C. (20 oz.)	6 C. (24 oz.)

Containers: 1-gallon freezer bags or 9x13 casserole

Assembly Directions:
To Pre-Bake on Cooking Day:
Brown the pork chops in a large skillet with the oil. Sprinkle them with salt and pepper (optional).
In a sprayed 9x13 baking dish, combine the water, rice, tomato sauce and taco seasoning; mix well.
Arrange the browned chops over the rice and top with green pepper. Cover and bake at 350° for 1 hour.
To Bake on Serving Day:
Brown FRESH pork chops in the oil. Cool and place in freezer container or bag. In a separate freezer bag
or container, place rice, water, tomato sauce and taco seasoning. Stir well in container and seal. Seal
cheese and pepper in separate bags. Label all bags and freeze.

Freezing and Cooking Directions:
Pre-Baked Casserole:
Remove from oven and cool. Wrap dish in freezer paper, or foil, or place dish in 2-gallon freezer bag. Put
shredded cheese in a small freezer bag and attach to the casserole dish. Seal, label, and freeze.
To serve, thaw casserole. Cover tightly with foil and bake at 350° for 15 minutes. Sprinkle cheese and
return to oven uncovered for 15 minutes.
Non-Baked Meal:
Tape all freezer bags together or put all in 2-gallon freezer bag.
To serve, thaw all bags. Pour contents of rice bag in sprayed 9x13 casserole. Arrange chops over rice.
Sprinkle pepper over chops. Cover with foil and bake at 350° for 1 hour. Top with cheese and bake
uncovered an additional 15 minutes.

Recipe: Breaded Fish Fillets

Meals:	1	2	3	4	5	6
serves 4-6						

Ingredients:

	1	2	3	4	5	6
fresh fish fillets	1-1/2 lbs.	3 lbs.	4-1/2 lbs.	6 lbs.	7-1/2 lbs.	9 lbs.
eggs	1	2	3	4	5	6
milk	1 T.	2 T.	3 T.	1/4 C.	1/4C.+1T.	1/4C.+2T.
fresh bread crumbs	1 C.	2 C.	3 C.	4 C.	5 C.	6 C.
salt	1/2 t.	1 t.	1-1/2 t.	2 t.	2-1/2 t.	1 T.
pepper	1/4 t.	1/2 t.	3/4 t.	1 t.	1-1/4 t.	1-1/2 t.

Containers: 1-gallon freezer bags or rigid freezer containers

Assembly Directions:
Mix egg and milk together in a shallow bowl. In another bowl combine crumbs, salt, and pepper. Dip fish in egg mixture then dredge in crumbs on both sides.

Freezing and Cooking Directions:
Place fish on a cake cooling rack that is set on a cookie sheet. Place baking sheet with cooling rack and coated fish in freezer. Freeze until firm. Place fish in a single layer in a freezer container or 1-gallon freezer bag. Label and put in freezer.
To serve, place frozen fish in a single layer on a sprayed or greased baking sheet. Bake 10 minutes at 450° or until opaque and flakes easily.

Recipe: West Country Cod

Meals:	1	2	3	4	5	6
serves 4-6						

Ingredients:

	1	2	3	4	5	6
white fish pieces	1-1/2 lbs.	3 lbs.	4-1/2 lbs.	6 lbs.	7-1/2 lbs.	9 lbs.
onion, chopped	1/2 C.	1 C.	1-1/2C.	2 C.	2-1/2C.	3 C.
butter/margarine	2 T.	1/4 C.	6 T.	1/2 C.	1/2C.+2T.	3/4 C.
cornstarch	3 T.	3/8 C.	1/2C.+1T.	3/4 C.	3/4C.+3T.	1C.+ 2T.
white cooking wine or apple juice	2 C.	4 C.	6 C.	8 C.	10 C.	12 C.
Dijon-type mustard	1 t.	2 t.	1 T.	1T.+1t.	1T.+ 2t.	2 T.
dried parsley	1 T.	2 T.	3 T.	1/4 C.	1/4C.+1T.	1/4C.+ 2T.

brown sugar to taste
salt and pepper to taste

Containers: 1-quart freezer bags or 8x8 casserole

Assembly Directions:
To Pre-Bake:
Roll up each fillet (if possible) and secure with a toothpick. Arrange the rolled fillets in an oiled, sprayed baking dish. Sprinkle the chopped onion over the fish. Melt butter/margarine in a saucepan. Stir in the cornstarch and cook for one minute, stirring constantly. Gradually stir in the juice or wine, mustard, parsley, brown sugar and seasoning. Bring to a boil, stirring constantly. Remove from heat and pour sauce over fillets. Bake fish at 375° for 10-15 minutes.
To Bake on serving day:
Leave fish frozen or if purchased fresh, put in 1-gallon freezer bags. Bag chopped onion. Prepare sauce as directed. Cool. Place sauce in freezer bag or container.

Freezing and Cooking Directions:
For Pre-Baked Casserole:
Cool. Carefully remove the picks and wrap in foil, or place in 2-gallon freezer bag. Label and freeze.
To serve, unwrap and thaw. Cover and bake at 375° until heated through (35-45 minutes). Taste and adjust seasoning.
For Freezer Bag Fish and Sauce:
Leave fish frozen or if purchased fresh, put in 1-gallon freezer bag. Cool sauce and put in quart-sized freezer bag. Put fish, sauce and onion inside a large freezer bag. Label and freeze.
To serve, thaw fish and sauce. Roll each fillet (if possible) and arrange in a sprayed baking dish. Sprinkle the chopped onion over the fish. Pour sauce over fillets. Bake fish at 375° until heated through (35-45 minutes). Taste and adjust seasonings.

Recipe: Citrus Marinade for Fish Fillets

Meals: serves 4-6	1	2	3	4	5	6
Ingredients:						
fish fillets, fresh or frozen	1-1/2 lbs.	3 lbs.	4-1/2 lbs.	6 lbs.	7-1/2 lbs.	9 lbs.
Marinade:						
lime juice	1/3 C.	2/3 C.	1 C.	1-1/3C.	1-2/3C.	2 C.
cooking oil	1 T.	2 T.	3 T.	1/4 C.	1/4C.+1T.	1/4C.+ 2T.
salt	1/4 t.	1/2 t.	3/4 t.	1 t.	1-1/4t.	1-1/2t.
water	1/3 C.	2/3 C.	1 C.	1-1/3C.	1-2/3C.	2 C.
honey (optional)	1 T.	2 T.	3 T.	1/4 C.	1/4C.+1T.	1/4C.+ 2T.
dill weed, dried	1/2 t.	1 t.	1-1/2t.	2 t.	2-1/2t.	1 T.

Containers: 1-gallon freezer bags or rigid freezer containers

Assembly Directions:
Combine marinade ingredients.

Freezing and Cooking Directions:
Pour marinade into equal freezer bags or rigid freezer containers. (Each meal equals approximately 3/4 C. marinade.) Seal, label and freeze. Seal fish fillets in a freezer bag and freeze.
To serve, thaw marinade and fish until completely softened. Place thawed fish fillets in thawed marinade for 10 minutes. Remove the fish from the marinade, reserving it for later. Place fish on greased broiler rack or grill. Tuck under any thin portion. Broil 4" from heat element, basting often with reserved marinade, until fish flakes easily. It takes just a few minutes, so watch carefully. Brush with marinade again just before serving. Discard any leftover marinade.

SIDE DISHES & MISC.

Cheese-Filled Shells

Wild Rice Dressing

Quiche in a Bag

Fruit Slush

Mexicali Casserole

California Pilaf

White Sauce

■ Tara's Macaroni & Cheese

■ Make Ahead Mashed Potatoes

■ Gramette's Dressing

■ Crispy, Cheesy Potatoes

■ Pasta with Herb Sauce

■ Champagne Salad

■ Fat Free White Sauce

TIPS FOR SIDE DISHES, SALADS, AND MISC.

General Tips For Sides, Salads, and Misc.
✓ Meats may be added to many of the side dishes in this section if you want to add protein.
✓ Cooked ground beef or sausage may be added to *Cheese Filled Shells.*
✓ Cooked ground or roast beef added to the *Mexicali Casserole* would make a great main dish.
✓ The sausage may be increased in the *Wild Rice Dressing* recipe.
✓ *Quiche In A Bag* could easily have ham or sausage added to it.
✓ Ham could also be included in *Tara's Macaroni and Cheese.*
✓ Many of these side dish recipes could be used as meatless main dishes.
✓ Many of these side dishes can be used as festive holiday dishes. Wouldn't it be great to have them ready in the freezer ahead of time?
✓ The *Make-Ahead Mashed Potatoes* also serve as a good top layer to many casseroles and thick stews.
✓ Many of these recipes make great, convenient picnic or potluck supper foods.
✓ All fresh vegetables except chopped onion, green pepper, and celery must be blanched before being added to foods going into the freezer. See page 131 in the *Appendix* for a vegetable blanching chart.
✓ 1 pound of fresh vegetables with little waste (green beans or carrots for example), or 2 pounds with shells or heavy peels (peas, beets, and winter squash for example) serves three to four adults.
✓ One 16 ounce can, or 10 ounces of frozen vegetables, serves three to four adults.

Healthy Tips For Sides, Salads, and Misc.
✓ Making these dishes ahead really helps to plan your "5 a day" servings of fruits and veggies!

✓ If you plan a potato side dish for your dinners (potatoes *are* a vegetable), a good vegetable or dark green salad, and one other raw or cooked vegetable, plus a frozen fruit salad for dessert, you will have had *four* of those servings - easy huh?

✓ Cutting down on meats is a good goal for many of us. Remember to try some of these side dish recipes as your main dish!

✓ We use whole wheat pastas, breads, and rice when assembling these recipes. This helps tremendously in getting enough fiber into our diets.

Cheese-stuffed shells is one of our favorites and a great sit-down job for the end of the day.

Recipe: Cheese-Filled Shells

Meals: serves 6-8	40 shells	80 shells	120 shells	160 shells	200 shells	240 shells
Ingredients:						
jumbo pasta shells	40 (12 oz. box)	80 (24 oz.)	120 (36 oz.)	160 (48 oz.)	200 (60 oz.)	240 (72 oz.)
cottage cheese	32 oz.	64 oz.	96 oz.	128 oz.	160 oz.	192 oz.
mozzarella cheese, shredded	16 oz.	32 oz.	48 oz.	64 oz.	80 oz.	96 oz.
grated parmesan cheese	3/4 C.	1-1/2C.	2-1/4C.	3 C.	3-3/4C.	4-1/2C.
eggs	3	6	9	12	15	18
oregano	3/4 t.	1-1/2t.	2-1/4t.	1 T.	1T.+3/4t.	1T.+1/2t.
salt (optional)	1/2 t.	1 t.	1-1/2t.	2 t.	2-1/2t.	1 T.
pepper	1/2 t.	1 t.	1-1/2t.	2 t.	2-1/2t.	1 T.
On Hand:						
*spaghetti sauce	28 oz. (3-1/2C.)	56 oz. (7 C.)	84 oz. (10-1/2C.)	112 oz. (14 C.)	140 oz. (17-1/2C.)	168 oz. (21 C.)

Containers: rigid containers for shells, freezer bags for homemade sauce

Assembly Directions:
Cook jumbo shells 1/2 of recommended time until just limp. Drain. Cool in a single layer on pan or waxed paper. Combine cheeses, eggs, oregano, salt and pepper. Fill each shell with 2 T. cheese mixture. *Tip: Using an icing bag with a wide tip works well for this or make your own by snipping the corner off a freezer bag.*

Freezing and Cooking Directions:
Freeze quantity of shells for one meal in a rigid container. Freeze homemade sauce in freezer bag.
To serve, thaw cheese-filled shells and sauce. Spread 1/2 C. spaghetti sauce in bottom of 9x13 baking dish. Arrange shells in dish. Pour remaining sauce over shells.   Warm at 350° for 30 minutes.

Comments:
Our kids really like these. They can be totally fat free or lower in fat depending upon your cheese, sauce, and egg choices. One recipe makes a lot, so you might divide it into two meals or one meal and a few lunches like we do.

*We buy whole wheat shells through our food cooperative (see page 139). You could also use manicotti shells.
*See our *Zippy Spaghetti Sauce* recipe on page 51. You can leave out the meat if you want a meatless dish.

Recipe: Wild Rice Dressing (with sausage added, it's a main dish!)

Meals: serves 4-6	1	2	3	4	5	6
Ingredients:						
*mild pork or turkey sausage(optional)	1/2 lb.	1 lb.	1-1/2 lb.	2 lb.	2-1/2 lb.	3 lb.
wild rice, cooked (dry)	2 C. (1/2 C.)	4 C. (1 C.)	6 C. (1-1/2C.)	8 C. (2 C.)	10 C. (2-1/2C.)	12 C. (3 C.)
celery, diced or sliced	1 C.	2 C.	3 C.	4 C.	5 C.	6 C.
onion, diced	1 C.	2 C.	3 C.	4 C.	5 C.	6 C.
poultry seasoning	1 T.	2 T.	3 T.	1/4 C.	1/4C.+1T.	1/4C.+2T.
turkey or chicken broth	1 C.	2 C.	3 C.	4 C.	5 C.	6 C.
brown sugar or molasses	1 T.	2 T.	3 T.	1/4 C.	1/4C.+1T.	1/4C.+2T.
parsley flakes	1 T.	2 T.	3 T.	1/4 C.	1/4C.+1T.	1/4C.+2T.
cranberries, chopped (fresh or frozen)	1/2 C.	1 C.	1-1/2C.	2 C.	2-1/2C.	3 C.
green apples, chopped	2 C.	4 C.	6 C.	8 C.	10 C.	12 C.
pecans or walnuts, chopped	3/4 C.	1-1/2C.	2-1/4C.	3 C.	3-3/4C.	4-1/2C.
wheat or white bread cubes, stale or dry	5 C.	10 C.	15 C.	20 C.	25 C.	30 C.

Containers: 1-gallon freezer bags or rigid freezer containers

Assembly Directions:
Cook and crumble pork or turkey sausage. Cook wild rice (thoroughly, this time!). In a skillet, saute the celery, onion, and poultry seasoning (this may be steam-sauteed in the microwave) until crisp tender. Add broth and brown sugar or molasses to celery mixture. Mix well. Add sausage (opt.), parsley flakes, cranberries, apples, nuts, bread cubes and rice. Mix well.

Freezing and Cooking Directions:
Place mixture in labeled freezer bags or rigid freezer containers. Freeze.
To serve, thaw completely and transfer dressing to a spray-treated or greased baking dish. Cover and bake at 350° for 45 minutes. Uncover and bake an additional 15 minutes.

Comments:
It's great to have this made and frozen for holiday or "special" meals. This dressing may be baked outside the bird or stuffed inside.
*Adding the sausage makes this a filling main dish entree.

Recipe: Quiche in a Bag

Meals:	1	2	3	4	5	6

serves 4-6

Ingredients:

	1	2	3	4	5	6
*meat, cooked (any meat diced or browned and crumbled)	1 C.	2 C.	3 C.	4 C.	5 C.	6 C.
vegetable (any *raw, blanched; thawed frozen; or canned, drained)	3/4 C.	1-1/2C.	2-1/4C.	3 C.	3-3/4C.	4-1/2C.
cheddar cheese, shredded	1 C.	2 C.	3 C.	4 C.	5 C.	6 C.
onion, diced	1/4 C.	1/2 C.	3/4 C.	1 C.	1-1/4C.	1-1/2C.
milk	2 C.	4 C.	6 C.	8 C.	10 C.	12 C.
eggs	4	8	12	16	20	24
Tabasco sauce	1/8 t.	1/4 t.	3/8 t.	1/2 t.	1/2t.+1/8t.	3/4 t.
flour (whole wheat works fine)	1/2 C.	1 C.	1-1/2C.	2 C.	2-1/2C.	3 C.
baking powder	2 t.	1T.+1t.	2 T.	2T.+2t.	3T.+1t.	1/4 C.

Containers: 1-gallon freezer bags

Assembly Directions:
Combine meat, vegetable, cheese, and onion. Place this mixture in a labeled 1-gallon freezer bag. With a mixer or blender, combine the milk, eggs, Tabasco sauce, flour and baking powder. Pour into the bag with the meat/vegetable mixture.

Freezing and Cooking Directions:
Seal and freeze. To serve, thaw completely. Shake bag well and pour into a spray-treated or greased deep dish pie plate or quiche pan. Sprinkle with paprika if desired. Bake at 350° for 35-45 minutes, until lightly browned on top and well set in the center. Cool about 5 minutes before serving.

Comments:
This is one of those dishes that you can get on the table when you haven't even looked in the freezer until 5:30 (like Nanci usually doesn't!). Just thaw the bag in the microwave, pour it in a dish, and pop it in the oven. Presto - dinner!

*For a vegetarian meal, just leave out the meat and increase the veggies by 1 C. for each recipe.
*See our Blanching Chart on page 131 if you are using fresh vegetables.

Recipe: Fruit Slush

Makes:	16 C.	32 C.	48 C.	64 C.	80 C.	96 C.
Ingredients:						
fruit cocktail, in syrup	40 oz.	80 oz.	120 oz.	160 oz.	200 oz.	240 oz.
strawberries; sliced, sweetened, frozen	10 oz.	20 oz.	30 oz.	40 oz.	50 oz.	60 oz.
orange juice concentrate, frozen	12 oz.	24 oz.	36 oz.	48 oz.	60 oz.	72 oz.
pineapple; crushed, in juice	20 oz.	40 oz.	60 oz.	80 oz.	100 oz.	120 oz.
bananas, diced	3	6	9	12	15	18

Containers: quart-sized freezer bags, small rigid freezer containers, or foil baking cups

Assembly Directions:
Partially thaw strawberries, so they can be separated. Mix all the ingredients together including all the juices from the canned and frozen fruits.

Freezing and Cooking Directions:
Pour into suitable containers for your family. Allow about 1/4-1/3 C. per child, 1/2 C. per adult. The leftovers have to be re-frozen, so make sure not to have *too* much leftover. Label and freeze.
To serve, thaw 10-15 minutes before needed - it should be slushy.

Comments:
Fresh fruits may be added to your liking. Small Styrofoam cups with lids may be purchased at restaurant supply stores. These work well for take out lunches. By lunchtime, they will be slushy and ready to eat!

Recipe: Mexicali Casserole

Meals: serves 4-6	**1**	**2**	**3**	**4**	**5**	**6**
Ingredients:						
onion, chopped	1 C.	2 C.	3 C.	4 C.	5 C.	6 C.
kidney beans, canned	16 oz.	32 oz.	48 oz.	64 oz.	80 oz.	96 oz.
white or brown rice, cooked 1/2 recommended time	2 C.	4 C.	6 C.	8 C.	10 C.	12 C.
tomatoes; diced or crushed, in *liquid* (not sauce)	28 oz.	56 oz.	84 oz.	112 oz.	140 oz.	168 oz.
corn, canned	15 oz.	30 oz.	45 oz.	60 oz.	75 oz.	90 oz.
OR						
corn, frozen	1-3/4C.	3-1/2C.	5-1/4C.	7 C.	8-3/4C.	10-1/2C.
pepper to taste						
cheese, shredded	2 C.	4 C.	6 C.	8 C.	10 C.	12 C.

Containers: 1-gallon freezer bags or rigid freezer containers

Assembly Directions:
Drain and reserve liquid from tomatoes. Drain water from canned corn. Drain kidney beans. Saute onion in a small amount of liquid from tomatoes. Add beans, cooked rice, tomatoes, and corn.

Freezing and Cooking Directions:
Pour into labeled freezer bags or rigid freezer containers. Place cheese in a separate freezer bag or container. Put both bags into a larger freezer bag. Freeze.
To serve, thaw completely. Pour rice mixture into spray treated 2-quart casserole. Sprinkle with cheese. Bake at 350° for 30 minutes or until heated thoroughly.

Comments:
Optional: *This dish could serve as a meatless main entree or 2-1/2 C. of cooked ground beef may be added to the casserole before freezing. It could then be used as a main dish.*

Recipe: California Pilaf

Meals: serves 6	1	2	3	4	5	6
Ingredients:						
quick cooking brown rice, uncooked	2 C.	4 C.	6 C.	8 C.	10 C.	12 C.
celery, diced	1 C.	2 C.	3 C.	4 C.	5 C.	6 C.
onion, diced	1/2 C.	1 C.	1-1/2C.	2 C.	2-1/2C.	3 C.
dry spaghetti, broken into 1" pieces	1/2 C.	1 C.	1-1/2C.	2 C.	2-1/2C.	3 C.
butter/margarine	1/4 C.	1/2 C.	3/4 C.	1 C.	1-1/4C.	1-1/2C.
chicken broth powder **OR**	2 T.	1/4 C.	1/4C.+2T.	1/2 C.	1/2C.+2T.	3/4 C.
bouillon granules	2 t.	1T.+1t.	2 T.	2T.+2t.	3T.+1t.	4 T.
parsley flakes	1 t.	2 t.	1 T.	1T.+1t.	1T.+2t.	2 T.
ground thyme	1/2 t.	1 t.	1-1/2t.	2 t.	2-1/2t.	1 T.
pepper	1/4 t.	1/2 t.	3/4 t.	1 t.	1-1/4t.	1-1/2t.
water	2 C.	4 C.	6 C.	8 C.	10 C.	12 C.

Containers: 1-gallon freezer bags or rigid freezer containers

Assembly Directions:
In a large skillet, saute the rice, celery, onion, and broken pasta in the butter. Stir constantly until the rice and pasta are golden brown. Stir in the parsley flakes, ground thyme and pepper. Cool. Stir in bouillon granules.

Freezing and Cooking Directions:
Place cooled rice mixture in labeled freezer bags or rigid containers. Seal and freeze.
To serve, thaw thoroughly. Place mixture in a saucepan or skillet with a lid. Stir in the water. Bring to a boil, then reduce heat to a simmer. Cover pan with a lid and cook for 10 minutes. Remove pan from heat and let stand for 10 minutes before serving.

Comments:
Options: *The water may be added and the pilaf fully cooked on Assembly Day. The pilaf could then be reheated quickly in the oven or microwave.*
This dish could serve as a meatless main entree or 2-1/2 C. of cooked meat may be added for a standard entree.

Recipe: Tara's Macaroni and Cheese

Meals:	1	2	3	4	5	6
serves 4						

Ingredients:

	1	2	3	4	5	6
macaroni, fully cooked	4 C.(cooked) (8-9 oz. dry)	8 C.	12 C.	16 C.	20 C.	24 C.
*white sauce	2 C.	4 C.	6 C.	8 C.	10 C.	12 C.
cream cheese, softened	4 oz.	8 oz.	12 oz.	16 oz.	20 oz.	24 oz.
sharp cheddar cheese, shredded	2 C.	4 C.	6 C.	8 C.	10 C.	12 C.
crackers, crushed or fresh bread crumbs	1/2 C.	1 C.	1-1/2C.	2 C.	2-1/2C.	3 C.

salt and pepper to taste

Containers: freezer bags, rigid freezer containers, or sprayed/greased casserole dishes

Assembly Directions:
Stir white sauce, a little at a time, into the softened cream cheese, removing any lumps as you stir. Mix in the shredded cheese and cooked macaroni. Salt and pepper to taste.

Freezing and Cooking Directions:
Label, and freeze in bags or rigid containers. Place crumbs in a small bag or container. Attach to macaroni and cheese or put both inside a large freezer bag. Seal and freeze.
To serve, thaw both bags or containers. Press macaroni mixture into greased or sprayed 1-1/2 to 2 quart baking dish. Sprinkle crumbs over macaroni. Bake at 375° for about 30 minutes until the edges are bubbly.

Comments:
Frozen vegetables like broccoli, chopped asparagus, or carrots may be stirred in on Assembly Day.
Fresh vegetables, including: carrots, onions, mushrooms, or peppers may be stirred in on the day you serve the dish.

*See our white sauce recipes on page 107 & 108.

Recipe: Make Ahead Mashed Potatoes

Makes:	7 C.	14 C.	21 C.	28 C.	35 C.	42 C.
Ingredients:						
potatoes	5 lbs.	10 lbs.	15 lbs.	20 lbs.	25 lbs.	30 lbs.
eggs	1	2	3	4	5	6
garlic powder	1/2 t.	1 t.	1-1/2t.	2 t.	2-1/2t.	1 T.
butter/margarine, melted	3 T.	1/4C.+2T.	1/2C.+1T.	3/4 C.	3/4C.+3T.	1C.+2T.
salt	1 t.	2 t.	1 T.	1T.+1t.	1T.+2t.	2 T.
cream cheese	8 oz.	16 oz.	24 oz.	32 oz.	40 oz.	48 oz.
almonds, sliced (optional)	1/4 C.	1/2 C.	3/4 C.	1 C.	1-1/4C.	1-1/2C.

paprika for color

Containers: quart or 1-gallon freezer bags or rigid freezer containers

Assembly Directions:
Peel and quarter potatoes. Place the potatoes in a saucepan and cover completely with water. Bring to a boil, then gently cook until tender. Drain well. In large bowl, combine potatoes, cream cheese, egg/s , garlic powder and salt. Mash well by hand or with an electric mixer. Spoon potatoes into spray-treated or greased 3 quart casserole or 9x13 pan. Drizzle or brush melted butter over potatoes. Sprinkle with almonds (optional) and paprika. Refrigerate for up to 2 days or label and freeze for later.

Freezing and Cooking Directions:
Label and freeze in freezer bags or rigid freezer containers.
To serve, thaw completely. Bake at 375° for 30-40 minutes until the top is golden.

Comments:
You'll love having this side dish handy. Our kids really love these (minus the almonds, of course!). Husbands, too.
Options: *1/4 C. crumbled, crisp bacon may be stirred in for great flavor.*
        **Potatoes may also be topped with 1/2 C. shredded cheddar cheese.*

Recipe: Gramette's Dressing

Meals:	1	2	3	4	5	6

serves 8-10

Ingredients:

	1	2	3	4	5	6
butter/margarine	1/4 C.	1/2 C.	3/4 C.	1 C.	1-1/4C.	1-1/2C.
celery, chopped	1 C.	2 C.	3 C.	4 C.	5 C.	6 C.
onion, chopped	1 C.	2 C.	3 C.	4 C.	5 C.	6 C.
sage, rubbed (to taste)	2 T.	1/4 C.	1/4C.+2T.	1/2 C.	1/2C.+2T.	3/4 C.
eggs	1	2	3	4	5	6
wheat bread and cornbread, stale or dried (homemade or purchased)	8 C.total	16 C.total	24 C.total	32 C.total	40 C.total	48 C.total
chicken or turkey broth	2-3 C.	4-6 C.	6-9 C.	8-12 C.	10-15 C.	12-18 C.

Containers: 1-gallon freezer bags or rigid freezer containers

Assembly Directions:

Melt butter in a large skillet. Saute onion and celery until tender in butter (this can be micro-steamed). Add the sage, then cool the mixture. Add the egg/s and mix well. Add cubed breads and toss until well coated. Gradually drizzle on the broth and toss until the dressing has reached a stage that it is a little soggier than you would want to see it on your plate (remember that some of the moisture will evaporate during baking).

Freezing and Cooking Directions:

Transfer dressing mixture to a labeled freezer bag or rigid freezer container. Seal and freeze.
To serve, bake covered in a sprayed or greased pan at 350° for 30 minutes, then raise the heat to 400° and bake uncovered for an additional 15 minutes until it is browned to your liking.

Comments:

Wouldn't it be great to serve homemade stuffing more than twice a year? You can't beat this recipe from Tara's mother-in-law!

*This dish could serve as a meatless main entree or 2-1/2 C. of cooked meat may be added for a standard entree.

Recipe: Crispy, Cheesy Potatoes

Meals: serves 6-8	1	2	3	4	5	6
Ingredients:						
hash browns; shredded, frozen	32 oz.	64 oz.	96 oz.	128 oz.	160 oz.	192 oz.
onion, chopped	1/4 C.	1/2 C.	3/4 C.	1 C.	1-1/4C.	1-1/2C.
sour cream	16 oz.	32 oz.	48 oz.	64 oz.	80 oz.	96 oz.
*white sauce, chicken flavored	1-1/2C.	3 C.	4-1/2C.	6 C.	7-1/2C.	9 C.
cheddar cheese, shredded	1-1/2C.	3 C.	4-1/2C.	6 C.	7-1/2C.	9 C.
corn flake cereal	2 C.	4 C.	6 C.	8 C.	10 C.	12 C.
butter/margarine, melted	1/3 C.	2/3 C.	1 C.	1-1/3C.	1-2/3C.	2 C.

Containers: 1-gallon freezer bags, rigid freezer containers or 9x13 pans

Assembly Directions:
Thaw the potatoes just slightly and break them apart well. Mix the onion, sour cream, white sauce, and cheddar cheese. Stir in half of the potatoes and mix well. Stir in the remaining potatoes. In another bowl or pan, melt the butter. Stir the corn flakes into the melted butter.

Freezing and Cooking Directions:
Press the potato mixture into a sprayed 9x13 baking pan or place in freezer bags or rigid containers.
Wrap pans with freezer paper or freezer weight foil or place pan into 2-gallon freezer bag and seal. Put the corn flake/butter mixture into a small freezer bag or container. Attach to the potato mixture.
Label both and freeze.
To serve, thaw potatoes and crumb topping. If frozen in bags or containers, put into a sprayed or greased 9x13 pan and top with the crumb mixture. Bake at 350° for 1 hour.

Comments:
Be sure to attach the crumbs to the bag somehow or you'll lose them! And yes, it is best to do the crumb topping now. Those corn flakes will never be there the day you need them, you know!
Mixing this in a LARGE pot or plastic tub with you hands is the quickest but you may get frostbite! Wear thick rubber gloves. They work great!
For a lower fat meal, use our Fat Free White Sauce along with lower or fat free sour cream and cheese.

*See our White Sauce recipes on page 107 & 108.

Recipe: Pasta with Herb Sauce

Serves:	6	12	18	24	30	36
Ingredients:						
Sauce:						
milk	1/4 C.	1/2 C.	3/4 C.	1 C.	1-1/4 C.	1-1/2 C.
grated parmesan cheese reduced fat or regular	1/4 C.	1/2 C.	3/4 C.	1 C.	1-1/4 C.	1-1/2 C.
ricotta cheese, low fat or regular	1/4 C.	1/2 C.	3/4 C.	1 C.	1-1/4 C.	1-1/2 C.
fresh parsley, chopped	1/4 C.	1/2 C.	3/4 C.	1 C.	1-1/4 C.	1-1/2 C.
green onions, sliced	2	4	6	8	10	12
dried basil leaves	2 t.	1T.+1t.	2 T.	2T.+2t.	3T.+1t.	4 T.
garlic, minced	1/2 t.	1 t.	1-1/2 t.	2 t.	2-1/2 t.	1 T.
Pasta:						
water	2 qts.	4 qts.	6 qts.	8 qts.	10 qts.	12 qts.
salt	1/2 t.	1 t.	1-1/2 t.	2 t.	2-1/2 t.	3 t.
fettucini or any pasta	6 oz.	12 oz.	18 oz.	24 oz.	30 oz.	36 oz.

Containers: 1-gallon freezer bags or rigid freezer containers

Assembly Directions:
Sauce: Puree the sauce ingredients together in a blender or food processor.
Pasta: Bring water to a boil. Add the salt and pasta. Bring back to a boil, then reduce the heat until it is gently bubbling and will not boil over. Cook pasta for a total of 8 minutes then drain it well. To serve without freezing, fully cook and drain the pasta, then toss the pasta with the sauce. Serve with grated parmesan cheese.

Freezing and Cooking Directions:
Freeze cooled, drained pasta in a labeled freezer bag or rigid freezer container. Place sauce in a smaller labeled container or bag and attach to pasta and vegetables, or place both components in a larger freezer bag. Freeze.
To serve, thaw both bags or containers thoroughly. Bring a - quart pot of water to a boil. Drop pasta into boiling water and cook to desired tenderness (about 5 minutes). Drain and stir in thawed sauce. Serve immediately, or too much of the sauce will soak into the pasta. Pass additional parmesan cheese at the table.

Comments:
Freshly boiled or steamed vegetables are very good stirred into the pasta. Try sliced carrots, broccoli florets, summer squash or snow

Recipe: Champagne Salad

Makes:	8 C.	16 C.	24 C.	32 C.	40 C.	48 C.
Ingredients:						
sugar	3/4 C.	1-1/2C.	2-1/4C.	3 C.	3-3/4C.	4-1/2C.
light cream cheese (at room temperature)	8 oz.	16 oz.	24 oz.	32 oz.	40 oz.	48 oz.
frozen, sliced strawberries; thawed	10 oz.	20 oz.	30 oz.	40 oz.	50 oz.	60 oz.
canned, crushed pineapple	20 oz.	40 oz.	60 oz.	80 oz.	100 oz.	120 oz.
bananas, diced	2	4	6	8	10	12
walnuts or pecans, chopped (optional)	1 C.	2 C.	3 C.	4 C.	5 C.	6 C.
*frozen whipped topping, thawed	10 oz.	20 oz.	30 oz.	40 oz.	50 oz.	60 oz.

Containers: Rigid, plastic containers with lids, 9x13 or other metal or glass dishes that can be covered with foil or freezer wrap. This salad may also be frozen in cupcake liners and placed in a freezer bag.

Assembly Directions:
Drain pineapple. In a large mixing container, cream the sugar and cream cheese together. Add strawberries, pineapple, bananas, and nuts (optional). Mix well. Fold in the whipped topping.

Freezing and Cooking Directions:
Spread in desired containers. Label and freeze.
To serve, thaw small portions 10-15 minutes before cutting into squares to serve, or large portions up to 30 minutes before serving.

Comments:
*4-5 Cups of real whipped cream may be substituted for the 10 oz. container of whipped topping.
*One recipe makes approximately 8 Cups of salad. Re-freeze leftovers.
*Try your own combinations of fruit. Even drained fruit cocktail, or melon balls would be good. Raspberries and blueberries work well because of their small size.
*If you want a less "sweet" salad, substitute 1-1/2 C. of sour cream for the whipped topping. (Fat free works very well.)
*Our husbands love this and our kids mostly do!

Recipe: White Sauce

Makes:	6 C.	12 C.	24 C.
Ingredients:			
butter/margarine or cooking oil (canola works fine)	3/4 C.	1-1/2 C.	3 C.
flour, (1/2 whole wheat is fine)	3/4 C.	1-1/2 C.	3 C.
milk, warmed	6 C.	12 C.	24 C.
chicken or beef flavoring:			
bouillon granules	2 T.	1/4 C.	1/2 C.
OR			
bouillon cubes	6	12	24
OR			
*broth powder	1/4 C.	1/2 C.	1 C.

Note: 1-1/2 C. of White Sauce = 1 small can (10-3/4 oz.) of soup.

Assembly Directions:
In a large, heavy bottomed or Teflon saucepan or stock pot, melt/warm the butter or oil over low heat. Add the flour and stir until the mixture is smooth. Cook the flour/oil mixture until it begins to bubble. Do NOT let it brown. Gradually add the milk, stirring CONSTANTLY. When the sauce has thickened (be patient; a 12-cup batch will take 30 minutes or so), stir in the bouillon granules, bouillon cubes, or the broth powder.

When making this sauce in more than 12-cup batches, it becomes difficult to keep from scorching it. We try to make 2 batches in different pans at once on different burners. It's a boring couple of hours of stirring (we usually make 60 cups each cooking day) but then it's all done and it is DELICIOUS!

Freezing and Cooking Directions:
When combined with other foods in casseroles, etc., this sauce freezes well. We would not recommend freezing it separately.

Comments:
We use this sauce or our Fat Free White Sauce any time white sauce is called for in one of our recipes. It is a great substitute for canned, creamed soups and saves money. If you use skim milk and canola oil, it is lower in fat and much better for your health, too. It can be seasoned with salt and pepper or other seasonings.

*To flavor our sauce, we always use a fat free, all natural broth powder (chicken or beef) that we order in bulk from our food cooperative. If you would like to order the broth powder directly from the company, you may call or write: Frontier Herbs
Box 299
Norway, IA 52318
(319)227-7991

Recipe: Fat Free White Sauce

Makes:	**6 C.**	**12 C.**	**24 C.**
Ingredients:			
flour, (1/2 whole wheat is fine)	1 C.	2 C.	4 C.
skim milk, warmed	6 C.	12 C.	24 C.
chicken or beef flavoring:			
bouillon granules	2 T.	1/4 C.	1/2 C.
OR			
bouillon cubes	6	12	24
OR			
*broth powder	1/4 C.	1/2 C.	1 C.

Note: 1-1/2 C. of White Sauce = 1 small can (10-3/4 oz.) of soup.

Optional: For more flavor and vitamins, add any of these finely minced vegetables: Sauteed or steamed onion, celery, mushrooms, broccoli.
Optional: For a cheese sauce, just add shredded cheddar, Swiss or grated parmesan cheese in desired amounts while sauce is still hot. Stir until melted.

Assembly Directions:
In a saucepan, warm 2/3 of the total amount of skim milk. Place all of the flour and broth flavoring in mixing bowl and gradually stir in the remaining 1/3 of the milk. When the milk/flour mixture is no longer lumpy, add it to the warm milk in the saucepan. Stirring constantly over medium, heat, bring the sauce to a gentle boil. Allow the sauce to boil one minute while continuing to stir. Remove saucepan from heat. Add any of the vegetable options.

Freezing and Cooking Directions:
When combined with other foods in casseroles, etc. this sauce freezes well. We would not recommend freezing it separately.

Comments:
We use this sauce or our White Sauce any time it is called for in one of our recipes. It is a great substitute for canned, creamed soups and saves money.
*To flavor our sauce we always use a fat free, all natural broth powder (chicken or beef) that we order in bulk from our Food Cooperative. If you would like to order the broth powder directly from the company, you may call or write: Frontier Herbs, Box 229, Norway, IA 52318 (319)227-7991
*We always make this a day or two before cooking day, as it is time consuming. To store easily, cool the sauce in a large roasting pan. Pour the sauce into large lidded pitchers, or pour the sauce (using a funnel) back into the plastic milk jugs, just to the point where the jug begins to angle back toward the cap. Replace the cap and refrigerate. The mixture will be thick – very similar to canned condensed creamed soups. To get at the mixture easily, use a sharp knife or kitchen shears to cut the top off of the jug, an inch or two above the sauce.
*This recipe's fat content depends on the amount of fat in the milk you choose and whether or not you steam or saute any added vegetables in oil. Cheese, of course, will also add to the fat content.

SNACKS & DESSERTS

- No-Bake Cookies
- Peanut Butter Balls
- Good-for-You Granola
- Breakfast McBiscuits
- Frozen Peanut Butter Bars

- Apple Squares
- Mozzarella Stix
- Snackin' Mix
- Stovetop Cereal Cookies
- Granola Bars

MASTER MIXES:

- Oatmeal Cookie Mix
- Master Baking Mix
- Quick Cobbler Mix

TIPS FOR SNACKS AND DESSERTS

Kids - ya gotta love'em! And we all do. But sometimes the *best* parents, grand-parents, and caregivers get weary just trying to keep up with the little darlings. Whether your children are in the up-at-night infancy stage, the picky "I want my way" toddler time, the wannabe indepen-dent elementary grades, or the so-busy-you-rarely-see-'em teenage years, YOU ARE BUSY and THEY ARE HUNGRY! Statistics about the health and eating habits of children in the United States are not encouraging. Kids today exercise less and are much heavier than they used to be. High cholesterol and high blood pressure are not uncommon among our youth! All the experts say that our child-ren need to eat more fruits and vegetables for fiber. We all want them to eat healthier, but how? So what's a parent to do? For us, part of the answer has come with bulk snack cooking. Like our 30 Day Gourmet dinner-time planning, we have found that having snacks readily available in the freezer keeps us from "drive-thru" snacking and saves us lots of money. The recipes included here are some of our kids' favorites. We tested over 50

Our favorite taste-testers!
Back: Hannah Wohlenhaus, Adam Slagle, Lydia Wohlenhaus
Middle: Katy Slagle, Becky Slagle, Estherre Wohlenhaus
Front: Jenna Slagle

healthy snacks on them (and a few neighbor kids!) and these were the winners. We hope you enjoy them too!

Healthy Tips For Snacks and Desserts

✓ Natural peanut butter is much better for the kiddos than the regular kind. Read the labels. Most peanut butters have the peanut oil removed and hydrogenated fats pumped in. Most also have sugar and salt added. We hope you will read the labels and be an informed food provider!

✓ Honey may be used in place of corn syrup in many recipes. Honey, however, has a stronger flavor. So you might buy the lightest color or clover honey which will be the mildest.

✓ Unsweetened applesauce can be substituted for up to 1/2 the oil in most recipes. Just be sure the recipe is not really high in fat in the first place, or the texture of the revised recipe may be disappointing.

✓ Whole-wheat flour is a good substitute for white flour whenever possible. The fiber and nutrients in the whole-wheat flour are great for our bodies! In baked goods, we generally use a mixture of 1/2 whole-wheat flour and 1/2 white flour. The kids rarely know the difference. If you choose to use whole-wheat flour, you need to refrigerate it if it will not be consumed within 30 days. The natural oil in the wheat germ is very perishable.

✓ Wheat germ is so good for all of us. It can be sprinkled into lots of recipes (cookies, breads, snack bars, etc.) without even tasting it. Try adding one tablespoon of raw or toasted wheat germ to each cup of flour or other dry ingredients.

✓ Try to make sure that the snacks your children eat have a redeeming nutritional value. If they are eating a snack loaded with butter or chocolate, what does it have in it that is good for the body? Oats, nuts, whole-wheat flour, raisins or other fruits can make a bad-for-you food into an acceptable food with a few added ingredients!

Recipe: No-Bake Cookies

Makes:	2 dz.	4 dz.	6 dz.	8 dz.	10 dz.	12 dz.
Ingredients:						
sugar	1 C.	2 C.	3 C.	4 C.	5 C.	6 C.
butter/margarine	1/4 C.	1/2 C.	3/4 C.	1 C.	1-1/4 C.	1-1/2 C.
cocoa powder	3 T.	1/4C.+2t.	1/2C.+1T.	3/4 C.	3/4C.+3T.	1C.+2T.
milk	1/4 C.	1/2 C.	3/4 C.	1 C.	1-1/4 C.	1-1/2 C.
peanut butter, creamy	1/3 C.	2/3 C.	1 C.	1-1/3 C.	1-2/3 C.	2 C.
oats, quick or regular	2 C.	4 C.	6 C.	8 C.	10 C.	12 C.
wheat germ (optional)	1/2 C.	1 C.	1-1/2 C.	2 C.	2-1/2 C.	3 C.
dry milk powder (optional)	1/2 C.	1 C.	1-1/2 C.	2 C.	2-1/2 C.	3 C.

Containers: rigid freezer containers

Assembly Directions:
In a saucepan, bring the sugar, butter, cocoa powder and milk together to a boil. As soon as it boils, remove it immediately from the heat and stir in the remaining ingredients. While still hot, drop by teaspoons onto waxed paper. Allow to cool and harden.

Freezing Directions:
Label and freeze in rigid containers.

Comments:
This is a healthier version of an age old favorite cookie. The kids will never notice the wheat germ or miss the extra butter.
*Use a cookie scoop for quicker and more uniform cookies.

Recipe: Peanut Butter Balls

Makes:	**2 dz.**	**4 dz.**	**6 dz.**	**8 dz.**	**10 dz.**	**12 dz.**
Ingredients:						
honey or corn syrup	1/3 C.	2/3 C.	1 C.	1-1/3C.	1-2/3C.	2 C.
peanut butter, creamy	1/2 C.	1 C.	1-1/2C.	2 C.	2-1/2C.	3 C.
dry milk powder	1 C.	2 C.	3 C.	4 C.	5 C.	6 C.
quick oats	1 C.	2 C.	3 C.	4 C.	5 C.	6 C.

Containers: rigid freezer containers or snack size freezer bags

Assembly Directions:
Mix honey or corn syrup and peanut butter in a bowl. Stir in oats (an electric mixer works well). Stir in just enough milk powder to help the balls hold their shape.   Roll in 24 balls.

Freezing and Serving Directions:
Place on plate or baking sheet and chill to eat now.
To eat later, freeze on tray until firm and place peanut butter balls in labeled freezer bags or rigid freezer containers.
To serve, thaw slightly, but keep chilled. These soften too much at room temperature to be practical for little hands!

Recipe: Good-for-You Granola

Makes:	12 C.	24 C.	36 C.	48 C.	60 C.	72 C.
Ingredients:						
whole wheat flour	2 C.	4 C.	6 C.	8 C.	10 C.	12 C.
rolled oats	6 C.	12 C.	18 C.	24 C.	30 C.	36 C.
coconut	1 C.	2 C.	3 C.	4 C.	5 C.	6 C.
wheat germ	1 C.	2 C.	3 C.	4 C.	5 C.	6 C.
water	1/2 C.	1 C.	1-1/2C.	2 C.	2-1/2C.	3 C.
oil	1 C.	2 C.	3 C.	4 C.	5 C.	6 C.
honey or corn syrup	1 C.	2 C.	3 C.	4 C.	5 C.	6 C.
vanilla extract	2 t.	1T.+1t.	2 T.	2T.+2t.	3T.+1t.	1/4 C.
salt	2 t.	1T.+1t.	2 T.	2T.+2t.	3T.+1t.	1/4 C.
Optional:						
sesame seeds	2 T.	1/4 C.	1/4C.+2T.	1/2 C.	1/2C.+2T.	3/4 C.
nuts	1/2 C.	1 C.	1-1/2C.	2 C.	2-1/2C.	3 C.
dried fruit	1 C.	2 C.	3 C.	4 C.	5 C.	6 C.

Containers: freezer bags, rigid freezer containers, or tightly sealed storage containers

Assembly Directions:
Combine dry ingredients in a large mixing bowl. Combine remaining ingredients in another bowl. If using nuts and/or seeds, add them to the dry ingredients. Combine the contents of both bowls and mix thoroughly. Spread mixture evenly on two spray-treated or greased large, rimmed cookie sheets. Bake at 250° for 1 hour, stirring twice during baking. Cool the store granola, and stir in dried fruit if desired. Store in airtight containers or freeze.

Freezing Directions:
Label and freeze.

Comments:
For out-of-hand snacking, leave the granola in a little larger clumps than you would for eating with a spoon. If you choose to add dried fruit, stir it in <u>after</u> baking and cooling granola thoroughly.

Recipe: Breakfast McBiscuits

Makes:	1 dz.	2 dz.	3 dz.	4 dz.	5 dz.	6 dz.

Ingredients:

Bread:

	1 dz.	2 dz.	3 dz.	4 dz.	5 dz.	6 dz.
*homemade biscuits	12	24	36	48	60	72
OR						
purchased refrigerator biscuits						
OR						
English muffins						

Meat:

	1 dz.	2 dz.	3 dz.	4 dz.	5 dz.	6 dz.
Pre-cooked bacon slices	24	48	72	96	120	144
OR						
ham slices	12	24	36	48	60	72
OR						
cooked sausage patties	12	24	36	48	60	72

Eggs:

	1 dz.	2 dz.	3 dz.	4 dz.	5 dz.	6 dz.
scrambled, fried, or poached	1 dz.	2 dz.	3 dz.	4 dz.	5 dz.	6 dz.
Cheese slices	12	24	36	48	60	72

Containers: rigid freezer containers or small freezer bags

Assembly Directions:
Split muffins or baked biscuits. Top with your choice of topping combinations.
Example: 2 slices of bacon, 1 egg, 1 slice of cheese OR
          1 sausage patty, 1 slice of cheese OR
          1/4 C. scrambled eggs, 1 slice of cheese
Be creative!

Freezing and Serving Directions:
Wrap individually, label, and freeze.
To serve, place thawed, foil-wrapped biscuit in oven and warm at 400° for 20 minutes or unwrap and re-wra
damp paper towel and microwave a few minutes.

Comments:
Large biscuits are more manageable than small ones. For purchased biscuits, choose the jumbo or extra large-s
variety. For homemade biscuits, don't overbake them or they will dry and crumble after reheating.
*See our Biscuit recipe in the Master Baking Mix on page 122.

Recipe: Frozen Peanut Butter Bars

Makes:	2 dz.	4 dz.	6 dz.	8 dz.	10 dz.	12 dz.
Ingredients:						
butter/margarine	1 C.	2 C.	3 C.	4 C.	5 C.	6 C.
peanut butter, creamy	2 C.	4 C.	6 C.	8 C.	10 C.	12 C.
*graham cracker crumbs	2-1/2 C.	5 C.	7-1/2 C.	10 C.	12-1/2 C.	15 C.
powdered sugar	1-3/4 C.	3-1/2 C.	5-1/4 C.	7 C.	8-3/4 C.	10-1/2 C.
chocolate chips, semi-sweet or milk chocolate	2 C.	4 C.	6 C.	8 C.	10 C.	12 C.
milk	1/3 C.	2/3 C.	1 C.	1-1/3 C.	1-2/3 C.	2 C.

Containers: freezer bags or rigid freezer containers

Assembly Directions:
In a large saucepan, melt butter and peanut butter together. Mix well. Remove from heat. Add crumbs and powdered sugar, mixing well. Spread peanut butter mixture in a jelly roll pan (for thinner bars) or 9x13 pan (for thicker bars). Chill. When the peanut butter layer is firm, melt chocolate chips with milk over low heat. Spread over chilled peanut butter mixture. Chill again.

Freezing Directions:
Cut into serving size pieces. Wrap individually and freeze in large rigid containers or freezer ziptop bags. Eat straight from the freezer or thaw slightly.

Comments:
Hey, you peanut butter and chocolate lovers! It doesn't get any better than this! If you can keep from eating them, these are great to keep around for company, after school snacking and for a treat after the kids go to bed!

We have found that we can usually buy the graham cracker crumbs for the same price as the equivalent in graham crackers. Why do the work if you don't have to?

30 DAY GOURMET
SNACK/DESSERT ENTREE

Recipe: Apple Squares

Makes:	24 sqs.	48 sqs.	72 sqs.	96 sqs.	120 sqs.	144 sqs.
Ingredients:						
flour	2 C.	4 C.	6 C.	8 C.	10 C.	12 C.
baking soda	1 t.	2 t.	1 T.	1T.+1t.	1T.+2t.	2 T.
cinnamon	1 t.	2 t.	1 T.	1T.+1t.	1T.+2t.	2 T.
salt	1/2t.	1 t.	1-1/2t.	2 t.	2-1/2t.	1 T.
oil	1 C.	2 C.	3 C.	4 C.	5 C.	6 C.
sugar	1-3/4C.	3-1/2C.	5-1/4C.	7 C.	8-3/4C.	10-1/2C.
eggs, beaten	4	8	12	16	20	24
vanilla	2 t.	1T.+1t.	2 T.	2T.+2t.	3T.+1t.	4 T.
apples; unpeeled, chopped	2 C.	4 C.	6 C.	8 C.	10 C.	12 C.
nuts, chopped (optional)	1/2 C.	1 C.	1-1/2 C.	2 C.	2-1/2 C.	3 C.
Frosting:						
powdered sugar	1-1/2 C.	3 C.	4-1/2 C.	6 C.	7-1/2 C.	9 C.
butter/margarine, melted	2 T.	1/4C.	1/4C.+2T.	1/2C.	1/2C.+2T.	3/4C.
water	3 T.	1/4C.+2T.	1/2C.+1T.	3/4 C.	3/4C.+3T.	1C.+2T.
vanilla	1 t.	2 t.	1 T.	1T.+1t.	1T.+2t.	2 T.

Containers: rigid freezer containers

Assembly Directions:
Stir together flour, baking soda, cinnamon, and salt. In another bowl, beat together oil, sugar, eggs, and vanilla. Add dry ingredients to liquid, beating well. Stir in apples and nuts (optional). Pour into spray-treated or greased 15½x10½x1" cookie sheet or jelly roll pan. Bake at 350° for about 30 minutes or until browned. Cool in pan. Mix all frosting ingredients together until smooth. Drizzle frosting over bars.

Freezing Directions:
Cut into squares. Label and freeze in rigid containers. Use waxed paper between layers.

Comments:
These are great to pull out for drop-in company and taste great at breakfast time, too!
Other fruits such as blueberries, drained pineapple, and sweet cherries may be substituted for the apples.
We have tried this using Egg Beaters to replace the eggs and apricot puree or applesauce to replace all of the oil. Tasted great!
If only a few of you like nuts, sprinkle the nuts over only 1/2 of the pan of batter before baking.

Recipe: Mozzarella Stix

Makes:	32 stix (3 inch)	64 stix	96 stix	128 stix	160 stix	192 stix
Ingredients:						
mozzarella sticks	16	32	48	64	80	96
eggs	2	4	6	8	10	12
water	1 T.	2 T.	3 T.	1/4 C.	1/4C.+1T.	1/4C.+2T.
dry, seasoned bread crumbs (purchased)	1 C.	2 C.	3 C.	4 C.	5 C.	6 C.
paprika	1/2 t.	1 t.	1-1/2t.	2 t.	2-1/2t.	1 T.
flour	3 T.	1/4C.+2T.	1/2C.+1T.	3/4 C.	3/4C.+3T.	1 C.+2 T.
On Hand: ***Spaghetti Sauce** (homemade or purchased)	1 C.	2 C.	3 C.	4 C.	5 C.	6 C.

Containers: Freezer bags or rigid freezer containers

Assembly Directions:
In a bowl, beat the eggs and water. Place the bread crumbs in a plastic bag. Coat the cheese sticks in flour, then dip in egg mixture and then shake in bread crumb coating.

Freezing and Cooking Directions:
Freeze on cookie sheets. When solid, place in freezer bags or rigid containers.
To serve, place frozen sticks on ungreased baking sheet and bake uncovered at 400° for 6-8 minutes or until thoroughly heated. Allow to set a few minutes before serving. Heat spaghetti sauce for dipping.

Comments:
Our kids really like these! The cheese sticks are very inexpensive at our discount grocery store or you can buy mozzarella cheese and cut it into 3x½" sticks.

*See our *Zippy Spaghetti Sauce* recipe on page 51.

Recipe: Snackin' Mix

Makes:	9 C.	18 C.	27 C.	36 C.	45 C.	54 C.
Ingredients:						
waffle-type cereal	7 C.	14 C.	21 C.	27 C.	35 C.	42 C.
dry roasted, mixed nuts or peanuts	1 C.	2 C.	3 C.	4 C.	5 C.	6 C.
pretzels	1 C.	2 C.	3 C.	4 C.	5 C.	6 C.
butter/margarine, melted	3 T.	6 T.	9 T.	12 T.	15 T.	18 T.
garlic salt	1/4 t.	1/2 t.	3/4 t.	1 t.	1-1/4t.	1-1/2t.
onion salt	1/4 t.	1/2 t.	3/4 t.	1 t.	1-1/4t.	1-1/2t.
lemon juice	2 t.	1T.+1t.	2 T.	2T.+2t.	3T.+1t.	1/4 C.
Worcestershire sauce	1 T.	2 T.	3 T.	1/4 C.	1/4C.+1T.	1/4C.+2T.

Containers: rigid freezer containers or snack size freezer bags

Assembly Directions:
Combine cereal, nuts and pretzels in 9x13 pan or large roasting pan. Set aside. Stir remaining ingredients together. Gently stir this mixture into cereal, nuts, and pretzels until evenly coated. Bake at 250° for 45 minutes, stirring every 15 minutes. Spread on paper towels to cool.

Freezing Directions:
Freeze in rigid containers to prevent crushing or in small quantity freezer bags for easy snacking. Mix may also be stored at room temperature in an airtight container or in food storage bags.

Comments:
The little snack size bags are so easy to grab for lunch boxes, car trips, or a quick outside snack!
*Use some of the wheat or multi-bran waffle type cereals for more fiber.
*After cooling, add small candy coated chocolates for color (and appeal!).
*Our recipe has less oil so it's safer in the mini-van!
*If mix becomes stale, it can be re-crisped for a few minutes in a 350° oven.
*Add small crackers (cheese or other varieties) in place of some of the pretzels if you like.

Recipe: Stovetop Cereal Cookies

Makes:	2 dz.	4 dz.	6 dz.	8 dz.	10 dz.	12 dz.
Ingredients:						
brown sugar	1/2 C.	1 C.	1-1/2C.	2 C.	2-1/2C.	3 C.
honey or corn syrup	1/4 C.	1/2 C.	3/4 C.	1 C.	1-1/4C.	1-1/2C.
vanilla extract	1 t.	2 t.	1 T.	1T.+1t.	1T.+2t.	2 T.
peanut butter, creamy	3/4 C.	1-1/2C.	2-1/4C.	3 C.	3-3/4C.	4-1/2C.
ready-to-eat cereal flakes	3 C.	6 C.	9 C.	12 C.	15 C.	18 C.
coconut (optional)	1 C.	2 C.	3 C.	4 C.	5 C.	6 C.

Containers: rigid freezer containers or snack size freezer bags

Assembly Directions:
Bring brown sugar and honey or corn syrup to a boil in a saucepan. Remove from heat. Stir in vanilla and peanut butter. Mix until smooth. Stir in cereal and coconut (optional). Drop by teaspoons onto waxed paper. Cool until firm.

Freezing and Serving Directions:
Put cookies into rigid freezer containers or snack size freezer bags and store in refrigerator or freezer.
To serve, thaw slightly, but keep chilled for firmness.

Recipe: Granola Bars

Makes:	16 bars	32 bars	48 bars	64 bars	80 bars	96 bars
Ingredients:						
vegetable oil	1/3 C.	2/3 C.	1 C.	1-1/3C.	1-2/3C.	2 C.
brown sugar	3/4 C.	1-1/2C.	2-1/4C.	3 C.	3-3/4C.	4-1/2C.
honey or corn syrup	2 T.	1/4 C.	1/4C.+2T.	1/2C.	1/2C.+2T.	3/4 C.
vanilla	1 t.	2 t.	1 T.	1T.+1t.	1T.+2t.	2 T.
eggs	1	2	3	4	5	6
whole wheat flour	1 C.	2 C.	3 C.	4 C.	5 C.	6 C.
cinnamon	1 t.	2 t.	1 T.	1T.+1t.	1T.+2t.	2 T.
baking powder	1/2 t.	1 t.	1-1/2t.	2 t.	2-1/2t.	1 T.
salt	1/4 t.	1/2 t.	3/4 t.	1 t.	1-1/4t.	1-1/2t.
oats	1-1/2C.	3 C.	4-1/2C.	6 C.	7-1/2C.	9 C.
crisp rice cereal	2 C.	4 C.	6 C.	8 C.	10 C.	12 C.
chopped nuts or sunflower seeds	1 C.	2 C.	3 C.	4 C.	5 C.	6 C.
Optional: raisins,	1 C.	2 C.	3 C.	4 C.	5 C.	6 C.

currants, chocolate chips, peanut butter chips, carob chips, chopped dried fruit, or a combo

Containers: snack size freezer bags for individual bars or rigid freezer containers

Assembly Directions:
In a large mixer bowl, combine oil, brown sugar, honey or corn syrup, vanilla, and egg. Add flour, cinnamon, baking powder, and salt. Mix well. With a large spoon, stir in oats, cereal, and nuts, fruits, or baking chips. Spray treat a 9x13 pan. Press the mixture evenly into bottom of pan. For chewy bars, bake at 350° for 20-30 minutes until lightly browned on the edges. For crunchy bars, bake at 300° until the surface is golden brown all over, about 40-50 minutes. Cool completely and cut into 16 bars by slicing through the middle lengthwise, then crosswise 7 times.

Freezing Directions:
Label and freeze in freezer bags or rigid freezer containers.

Comments:
This version of the supermarket standard is very good and very close to the name brands! Great for lunches and healthy snacking. Experiment with the options!

Recipe: Oatmeal Cookie Mix

Makes:	32 C. Mix	64 C. Mix	96 C. Mix	128 C. Mix	160 C. Mix	192 C. Mix
Ingredients:						
granulated sugar	3 C.	6 C.	9 C.	12 C.	15 C.	18 C.
brown sugar	3 C.	6 C.	9 C.	12 C.	15 C.	18 C.
flour	6 C.	12 C.	18 C.	24 C.	30 C.	36 C.
salt	1-T.+1t.	2-T.+2t.	1/4 C.	1/4C.+4t.	1/2 C.	1/2C.+4t.
baking soda	1T.+1t.	2T.+2t.	1/4 C.	1/4C.+4t.	1/2 C.	1/2C.+4t.
baking powder	2 t.	1T.+1t.	2 T.	2T.+2t.	3T.+1t.	1/4 C.
shortening	4 C.	8 C.	12 C.	16 C.	20 C.	24 C.
oats (any)	12 C.	24 C.	36 C.	48 C.	60 C.	72 C.
To Make:	**3 dz.**	**6 dz.**	**9 dz.**	**12 dz.**	**15 dz.**	**18 dz.**
eggs	2	4	6	8	10	12
vanilla	2 t.	1T.+1t.	2 T.	2T.+2t.	3T.+1t.	1/4 C.
cookie mix	4 C.	8 C.	12 C.	16 C.	20 C.	24 C.

Containers: 1 or 2 gallon freezer bags or tightly sealed rigid containers

Assembly Directions:
In large tub, mix first six ingredients with hand mixer or by hand. Cut in shortening with hand mixer. Stir in rolled oats. Place in airtight container if not baking now. Store mix in cool place.

Cooking Directions:
To use mix, combine the mix with the eggs and vanilla. Drop by teaspoonfuls onto baking sheets. Bake at 350° for 10-12 minutes.

Comments:
The cookies may be baked now and frozen, the dough can be frozen in a lump or open frozen in balls for individual cookies, or you can store the dry mix. Nuts, raisins, sunflower seeds, chocolate chips, etc., can be added with the oats or added just before the eggs and vanilla (if storing the dry mix). For all the variations (except chocolate chips) a teaspoon of cinnamon for each batch may be stirred into the eggs.Having the dry mix made up puts fresh-baked cookies in your families' hands in just a few minutes. It's SO easy!!

Recipe: Master Baking Mix

Makes:	20-25 C.	40-50 C.	60-75 C.
Ingredients:			
whole wheat pastry flour, or all purpose flour, or a mix	20 C. (5 lbs.)	40 C. (10 lbs.)	60 C. (15 lbs.)
baking powder	3/4 C.	1-1/2 C.	2-1/4 C.
salt	3 T.	1/4 C.+2 T.	1/2 C.+1 T.
cream of tartar	1 T.	2 T.	3 T.
sugar	1/2 C.	1 C.	1-1/2 C.
dry milk powder (optional)	4 C.	8 C.	12 C.

Optional: Add up to 2 C. wheat germ to each recipe. The dry milk powder is optional; it adds protein to the product. You can replace a cup or two of the flour with soy flour for even higher protein counts.

Containers: 1 or 2 gallon freezer bags or rigid freezer containers

Assembly Directions:

Sift all the ingredients together at least three times, or stir with a large spoon VERY well. Store in a covered container at room temperature. Label. If it contains whole wheat flour or wheat germ and it will not be used within a month or two, store it in the refrigerator.

Muffins:
Preheat oven to 425°. In a bowl, stir together:
1 C. milk or buttermilk   1 egg
2 T. sugar   3 T. oil
3 T. applesauce
Add 2-1/2 C. *Master Baking Mix.* Stir just until moistened. Spoon into greased muffin tins or paper liners and bake for 20 minutes. Makes 1 dozen. One cup of dried fruit bits, fresh or frozen blueberries, or nuts may be added to the dry ingredients before adding the liquids. If you prefer, use a total of 6 T. oil and omit the applesauce.

Quick Bread:
Combine ingredients as for muffins. Pour into a greased 5x8 loaf pan and bake at 350° for 40-45 minutes. Great toasted, too! Option: Mash 2 bananas and use only 3/4 C. of milk to make banana bread. A teaspoon of vanilla or coconut extract may be added also.

Biscuits:
Preheat oven to 450°. In a bowl, cut 1/4 C. shortening into 1-3/4 C. *Master Baking Mix.* Stir in 1/3 C. of milk all at once. Stir about 20 strokes and knead lightly on a floured board. Roll 1/2" thick and cut into shapes with a floured biscuit cutter. Bake on an ungreased baking sheet for 10 minutes.

Drop Biscuits:
Mix as for regular biscuits but increase the milk to 3/4 C. Drop by heaping Tablespoons onto greased baking sheets. 1 cup of shredded cheddar cheese and 1/4 t. garlic powder may be added to make a bread VERY similar to that found in a famous seafood restaurant named for a red crustacean similar to a crab.

Pancakes/ Waffles:
2 C. mix added to 1 egg, 1 C. of milk, 1 T. oil, beaten together. Yields 8 – 5" pancakes.

Recipe: Quick Cobbler Mix

Makes: serves 4-6	1	2	3	4	5	6
Ingredients:						
sugar	1 C.	2 C.	3 C.	4 C.	5 C.	6 C.
flour	1 C.	2 C.	3 C.	4 C.	5 C.	6 C.
baking powder	2 t.	1T.+1t.	2 T.	2T.+2t.	3T.+1t.	1/4 C.
salt	1/2 t.	1 t.	1-1/2 t.	2 t.	2-1/2 t.	1 T.
On Hand:						
milk	1 C.	2 C.	3 C.	4 C.	5 C.	6 C.
fruit; fresh, frozen, or canned	2 C.	4 C.	6 C.	8 C.	10 C.	12 C.

Containers: rigid freezer containers or freezer bags

Assembly Directions:
To Pre-Bake:
Combine sugar, flour, baking powder, and salt in a bowl. Stir in the milk and pour the mixture into a spray-treated 9x9 pan or baking dish. Add the fruit to the top, distributing evenly. Bake at 350° for 30-40 minutes until the top is browned. It looks odd but the crust will rise to the top. Cool.
To Bake on Serving Day:
Mix dry ingredients and store in an airtight container. To bake, measure out 2 C. of the dry mix. Stir in 1 C. milk. Pour the mixture into a spray-treated 9x9 pan or baking dish. Add the fruit to the top, distributing evenly. Bake at 350° for 30-40 minutes until the top is browned. The crust will rise to the top. Serve warm.

Freezing and Serving Directions:
Pre-Baked Cobbler: Thaw completely. Reheat in oven or microwave.

Comments:
We prefer to mix and store the dry ingredients and bake the cobbler fresh. It's really quick as long as you have milk and fruit on hand! The kids can even do this one!
Quick Cobbler is fat free (with skim milk) and tastes great for breakfast or dessert.
1 recipe will fit in an 8x8 or 9x9 baking dish.
2 recipes will fit in a 9x13 pan.

APPENDIX

EQUIVALENCY CHART

DRY MEASURE

Pinch = a little less than 1/4 teaspoon
3 teaspoons = 1 Tablespoon
2 T. = 1 oz. = 1/8 C.
4 T. = 2 oz. = 1/4 C.
5-1/3 T. = 2.7 oz. = 1/3 C.
8 T. = 4 oz. = 1/2 C.
10-2/3 T. = 5.4 oz. = 2/3 C.
12 T. = 6 oz. = 3/4 C.
16 T. = 8 oz. = 1 C.
4 C. = 1 quart
4 quarts = 1 gallon

LIQUID MEASURE

3 teaspoons = 1 Tablespoon
a dash = a few drops
2 T. = 1 oz.
4 T. - 2 oz. = 1/4 C.
5-1/3 T. = 2.7 oz. = 1/3 C.
8 T. = 4 oz. = 1/2 C.
10-2/3 T. = 6 oz. = 3/4 C.
16 T. = 8 oz. = 1 C.
2 C. = 1 pint = 1/2 quart
4 C. = 2 pints = 1 quart
4 quarts = 16 C. = 1 gallon = 128 oz.

DRY GOODS

Bread Cubes and Crumbs
4 slices of bread = 2 C. fresh soft crumbs
4 slices of bread = 3/4 C. dry crumbs
6 oz. dried bread crumbs = 1 scant cup
16 oz. loaf = 14 C. one inch cubes

Cereal Crumbs
16 oz. corn flake cereal = 5 quarts
2 C. flakes = 3/4 C. crumbs
21 oz. box corn flakes = 7 C. of cereal
15 oz. box puffed rice = 11 cups of cereal

Flours/Meal
1 lb. white flour = 3-1/2 C. or 4 C. sifted
1 lb. whole wheat flour = 3-1/4 C.
1 lb. whole wheat flour, sifted = 3-1/2 C.
1 C. flour = 4 oz.
14 oz. cracker meal = 3-3/4 C.

Leavening Agents
16 oz. baking soda = 2-1/3 C.
16 oz. baking powder = 2-1/3 C.
14 oz. can baking powder = 1-3/4 C.
5-1/2 oz. baking powder = 1 C.
.25 oz. active dry yeast = 1 T.
1 oz. of active dry yeast = 3-1/3 T.
16 oz. of active dry yeast = 3-1/3 C.
.60 oz. compressed yeast = 4 t.

Cooking Oil   8 oz. = 1 C.

Cracker Crumbs
28 soda crackers = 1 C. fine crumbs
16 oz. crackers = 6 C. fine crumbs = 8 C. coarse crumbs
15 square graham crackers = 1 C. crumbs
16 oz. graham crackers = 70 crackers
1 roll of snack crackers = about 1-1/3 C. crumbs
16 oz. of snack crackers = about 5-1/3 C. crumbs
24 round butter crackers = 1 C. fine crumbs
14 oz. box of cracker meal = 3-3/4 C. crumbs

Butter/Margarine/Shortening
1 T. = 1/2 oz. = 1/8 stick
4 T. = 2 oz. = 1/4 C. = 1/2 stick
8 T. = 4 oz. = 1/2 C. = 1 stick
16 T. = 8 oz. = 1 C. = 2 sticks
32 T. = 16 oz. = 2 C. = 4 sticks = 1 lb.
3 lb. can of shortening = 6 C.

Sweeteners
12 oz. honey = 1 C.
16 oz. honey = 1-1/2 C.
16 oz. corn syrup = 1-1/2 C.
11 oz. molasses = 1 C.
11 oz. maple syrup = 1 C.
16 oz. white sugar = 2-1/3 C.
16 oz. brown sugar = 2-1/4 C. packed
16 oz. powdered sugar = 3-1/2 C.
2/3 C. honey = 1 C. sugar + 1/3 C.

COMMERCIALLY CANNED FOODS

6 oz. can = about 3/4 C.
8 oz. can = about 1 C.
10.5 oz. can = about 1-1/4 C.
14.5 oz. can = about 1-2/3 C.
15.5 oz. can = about 1-3/4 C.
16 oz. can = about 2 C.
20 oz. can = 2-1/2 C.
46 oz. can juice = 5-3/4 C.

COMMERCIALLY FROZEN FOODS

1 oz. frozen vegetables = about 3 T. cooked
4 oz. frozen vegetables = about 3/4 C. cooked
5 oz. frozen vegetables = about 1 C. cooked
10 oz. frozen vegetables = about 2 C. cooked
16 oz. frozen vegetables = about 2-3/4 C. cooked
20 oz. frozen vegetables about 4 C. cooked

CAN SIZE EQUIVALENTS

Can Size	Measure Amount	Approximate Weight
No. 1	1-1/4 C.	10-1/2 oz.
No. 300	1-3/4 C.	15-1/2 oz.
No. 303	2 C.	16 oz.
No. 2	2-1/2 C.	24 oz.

DAIRY PRODUCTS

Shredded and Cubed Cheese
16 oz. = 4 C. cubed or shredded
4 oz. = 1 C. cubed or shredded
Heavy Whipping Cream
1 C. or 8 oz. carton = 2 C. whipped
Parmesan or Romano, grated
6 oz. = 1 C.
16 oz. = 2-2/3 C.
24 oz. = 3 C.
Cottage Cheese
6 oz. = 1 C.
16 oz. = 2-2/3 C.
Sour Cream
16 oz. = 1-3/4 C.
9 oz. = 1 C.
Cream Cheese
8 oz. = 1 C.
3 oz. = 6 T. or about 1/3 C.
1 lb. = 2 C.
Sweetened Condensed Milk
14 oz. can = 1-1/4 C.
Evaporated Milk
14-1/2 oz. can = 1-2/3 C.
6 oz. = 2/3 C.
1 C. = 3 C. whipped volume
Dry Milk Powder
16 oz. = 4 cups dry or 4-5 quarts of liquid
Buttermilk powder
12 oz. = 3-3/4 quarts of liquid buttermilk
1/4 C. buttermilk powder = 1 C. buttermilk

MEATS

Bacon
8 slices = 1/2 C. cooked and crumbled
16 oz. = about 18 slices
Beef
1 lb. ground = 2 1/2 C. browned
10 lbs. ground = 25 C. browned
1 lb. raw = 3-1/2 C. sliced = 3 C. cubed
Bulk Sausage
1 lb. raw = 2-1/2 C. cooked and crumbled
Chicken; boneless, skinless
7-1/2 lbs. raw = about 25 pieces
1 lb. raw = 2 C. raw ground = 2-2/3 C. raw diced
5 lbs. raw = 12 C. cooked, diced
1 large breast = 3/4 C. cooked, diced
2-1/2 lbs. = 7-8 large pieces
Chicken Thighs
5 lbs. = about 25 pieces
Whole Chicken
2-1/2 lb. chicken = 2-1/2 C. cooked meat off the bone
3-1/2 to 4 lb. chicken = 4 C. cooked meat off the bone
4-1/2 lb. 5 lb. chicken = 6 C. cooked meat off the bone
Crab meat (real or imitation)
1 lb. cooked and boned meat = 2 cups
Ham
1 lb. whole ham = 2-1/2 C. ground ham
1 lb. whole ham = 3 C. cubed
Turkey Breast
5 lb. raw breast = 10 C. cooked meat off the bone
1 lb. Drumstick or thigh = 1-1/8 C. diced cooked meat
Whole Turkey
Each lb. of turkey = approximately 1 C. cooked meat
Tuna Fish
6 oz. = 3/4 C. lightly packed

FRUITS

Apples
1 medium = 1 C. chopped
1 lb. = 3 medium
Strawberries/Raspberries
1 pint = 1-3/4 C.
4 oz. = 1 C.
Blueberries
1 lb = 3 C.

Applesauce
16 oz. = 2 C.
Bananas
1 lb.=3 med.=2-1/2 C. diced or 3 C. sliced
1 medium = 1/3 C. mashed
Pineapple
1 lb. = 2-1/2 C. diced

Lemons
1 medium = 3 T. juice
1 medium = 3 T. grated rind
5-8 lemons = 1 C. fresh juice
Oranges
1 = 1/3 C. fresh juice

MISCELLANEOUS

Jams/Jellies/Preserves
6 oz. = 2/3 C.
10 oz. = about 1 C.

16 oz. = 1-1/2 C.
16 oz. = 94 t. = 32 T. = 2 C.

Cocoa Powder
8 oz. = 2 C.
16 oz. = 4 C.
Chocolate Chips
6 oz. = 1 C.
Ketchup
28 oz. = 2-1/2 C.

Ice Cubes
11 cubes = 1 C. liquid
Mayonnaise
1 quart = 32 oz. = 4 C.
Nuts
16 oz. = 4 C.
2 oz. = 1/2 C.

Shredded Coconut
16 oz. = 5 C.
14 oz. = 3-1/4 C.
Peanut Butter
16 oz. = 1-3/4 C.

THICKENING AGENTS

1 T. cornstarch = 2 T. flour = 1 T. arrowroot powder = 1 T. tapioca flour = 1 T. Instant Clear Gel

ONE OUNCE OF WEIGHT TO MEASUREMENT OF HERBS AND SPICES

Allspice, ground	5-1/2 T.	Ginger	6 T.	Black Pepper; ground	1/2 C.
Basil	1/2 C.	Sesame Seed	5 T.	Chili Pepper	1/2 C. + 1-1/2 t.
Bay Leaf, whole	7 T.	Marjoram	1/2 C.	Red Pepper Flakes	1/2 C. + 1-1/2 t.
Celery Seed	1/4 C.	Mustard; dry, ground	6 T. + 1 t.	Poppy Seeds	3-3/4 T.
Cinnamon	5-1/2 T.			Rosemary	1/2 C.
Cloves, ground	5-1/2 T.	Nutmeg; ground	5 T.	Sage	1/2 C. + 1-1/2 T.
Cumin Seed	6 T.	Onion Powder	4-1/2 T.	Savory	6-3/4 T.
Curry Powder	5-1/2 T.	Oregano	6 T.	Sesame Seed	5 T.
Dill Weed	6 T.	Paprika	5 T.	Tarragon	6-3/4 T.
Dill Seed	4-1/2 T.	Parsley Flakes	1/2 C.+1-1/2 t.	Thyme	6-1/3 T.
Garlic Powder	6-1/3 T.			Turmeric	5 T.

VEGETABLES

Carrots
1 lb. = 3 C. sliced = 2 C. diced = 6-8 medium
1 medium carrot = 1/2 C. grated

Cooking Onions
1 lb. = 3 medium = 3 C. sliced or chopped
1 medium onion = 1 C. chopped
1 C. chopped = 1 T. dried, minced
1 C. chopped = 1 teaspoon powdered
1 medium onion = 2/3 C. sautéed

Green Onion
7 medium green onions = 1/2 C. sliced

Green Beans
1 lb. Fresh = 3 C. = 2-1/2 C. cooked

Celery
1 medium bunch = 4 to 5 C. diced
1 medium bunch = 2-1/2 to 3 C. sautéed
1 medium bunch = 3 C. diced = 3-1/2 C. sliced
3 large ribs = about 1-1/2 C. diced
1 Cup diced = 2/3 C. sautéed
1 rib = 1/2 C. sliced or diced

Corn
2-3 fresh ears = 1 C. kernels

Peas
4 oz. = 1 Cup

Potatoes
1 lb. = 3 medium = 2-3/4 C. diced = 3 C. sliced
1 lb. = 2 C. mashed
5 lbs. = 10 C. diced = 10 C. mashed

Sweet Potatoes
1 lb. = 3 medium = 2-1/2 to 3 diced

Spinach and other greens
1 lb. raw = 10-12 C. torn = 1 C. cooked
10 oz. frozen = 1-1/2 lb. Fresh = 1-1/2 C. cooked

Sweet Bell Peppers
1 medium = 1/2 C. finely chopped
1 lb. = 5 medium or 3-1/2 C. diced

Tomatoes
1 lb. = 4 small = 1-1/2 C. cooked

Cabbage
1 lb. = 4 - 5 C. shredded

Cauliflower
1 lb. = 1-1/2 C. cooked

Tomato sauce
8 oz. = 1 scant cup

Garlic
1 medium clove = 1/8 t. garlic powder
1 medium clove = 1/2 t. minced

Water Chestnuts
8 oz. sliced = 1 C. drained
8 oz. whole = 1 C. drained

Fresh Parsley
1 lb. = 6 C. chopped

Mushrooms
4 oz. fresh = 1 C. whole = 1/2 C. cooked
1 lb. = about 20 large or 40 medium whole
1 lb. = about 4 C. whole = 2 C. cooked

DRY BEANS/GRAINS/PASTA/NUTS

Lentils
6 oz. dry = 1 C.

Kidney Beans
11 oz. dry = 1 C. dry = 3 C. cooked
15 oz. can = 1-3/4 C.
16 oz. dry = 5 C. cooked

Barley
3/4 C. pearl barley = 3 C. cooked
1 C. quick cooking barley = 2-1/2 C. cooked

Long Grain White Rice
16 oz. dry = 2-1/2 C. dry = 10 C. cooked
1 C. dry = 7 oz. dry = 3 C. cooked

Quick Cooking Brown Rice
1 C. dry = 2 C. cooked
12 oz. box = 5-1/3 C. fully cooked
      = 4-1/2 C. half cooked

White Converted Rice
1 C. dry = 4 C. cooked

Oatmeal
42 oz. (2 lb. 10 oz. can) = 15 C. cooked oats
1 lb. = 4-5 C. dry
1 C. dry = 3 oz. dry = 1-3/4 C. cooked

Spaghetti
2 oz. = 1 serving = 1/2" diameter dry portion
8 oz. = 4-5 C. dry = 10 C. cooked

Elbow Macaroni
4 oz. dry = 1 C. dry = 2-1/2 C. cooked
16 oz. dry = 4 C. dry = 9 C. cooked

Egg Noodles
4 oz. dry = 1 C. dry = 3 C. cooked
16 oz. dry = 4 C. dry = 12 C. cooked

Tiny Pasta (acini pepe, orzo, ditalini, alphabets)
8 oz. dry = 1-1/3 C. dry

U.S. TO METRIC CONVERSIONS
FAHRENHEIT TO CENTIGRADE CONVERSIONS

VOLUME

United States Volume	Metric Volume
1 teaspoon (t or tsp.)	5 ml
2 teaspoons	10 ml
1 tablespoons (T or Tblsp.)	15 ml
2 tablespoons	30 ml
3 tablespoons	45 ml
1/4 cup (C)	60 ml
1/3 cup	80 ml
1/2 cup	120 ml
2/3 cup	160 ml
3/4 cup	180 ml
1 cup	240 ml
2 cups	480 ml
3 cups	720 ml
1 quart (qt)	950 ml
2 quarts	1.9 L
3 quarts	2.9 L
1 gallon	3.8 L

WEIGHT

U.S. Weight	Metric Weight
1/2 ounce (oz.)	14 g
1 ounce	28 g
2 ounces	56 g
4 ounces	114 g
8 ounces	227 g
1 pound (lb. Or #)	454 g
2 pounds	908 g
4 pounds	1.8 kg
5 pounds	2.3 kg
10 pounds	4.54 kg

TEMPERATURE

Fahrenheit Temperature	Centigrade Temperature
212	100
225	106
250	120
275	134
300	147
325	161
350	175
375	189
400	202
425	216
450	230
475	244
500	257

FREEZING TIME CHART

The following list should give you a good idea of the basics when freezing most ingredients used in **30 DAY GOURMET** cooking. Your local library probably has some very good books that are totally devoted to freezing which are great references. And remember not to skimp while wrapping foods for the freezer. If you use plastic ziptop bags, buy only the ones designed especially for freezing. Freezer wrap works quite well, too and can usually be re-used if you're one of those "saver types". To determine how long to freeze a recipe that has a combination of different ingredients, the item that freezes well the least amount of time is how long to freeze the entire recipe.

FOOD	FREEZER LIFE	FOOD	FREEZER LIFE
Baked Goods:		**Beef:**	
Bread dough; yeast, unbaked	2 weeks	raw ground beef/stew beef	3-4 months
Baked bread	12 months	fresh beef steak	6-12 months
Rolls:		fresh beef roast	6-12 months
unbaked	2 weeks	fresh beef sausage	3-4 months
1/2 baked	12 months	smoked beef links or patties	1-2 months
fully baked	12-15 months	cooked beef dishes	2-3 months
Muffins:		fresh beef in marinade	2-3 months
unbaked	2 weeks		
baked	3 months	**Pork:**	
Waffle/pancake batter	2-4 weeks	ground pork	3-4 months
Waffles/pancakes, cooked	6 months	fresh pork sausage	1-2 months
		fresh pork chops	4-6 months
		fresh pork roast	4-6 months
Dairy Products		bacon	1 month
Butter:		pepperoni	1-2 months
salted	3 months	smoked pork links or patties	1-2 months
unsalted	6 months	canned ham	don't freeze
Margarine	5 months	ham, fully cooked	
Hard cheese	3 months	whole:	1-2 months
Cream cheese	3 months	half or slices:	1-2 months
Milk	1 month	pre-stuffed pork chops	don't freeze
Eggs, raw and out of shell	6 months	cooked pork chops	2-4 months
		uncooked casseroles w/ham	1 month
		cooked casseroles w/ham	1 month
Produce		fresh pork in marinade	2-3 months
All Vegetables	12 months		
Exceptions:		**Poultry:**	
Asparagus	8-12 months	fresh ground turkey	2-3 months
Onions	6 months	fresh turkey sausage	1-2 months
Jerusalem artichokes	3 months	fresh whole turkey	12 months
Potatoes	3-6 months	chicken or turkey:	
Beets	6 months	fresh pieces	9 months
Green beans	8-12 months	cooked pieces	4 months
Leeks	6 months	cooked pieces covered w/broth	6 months
Winter squash	10 months	or gravy	
Mushrooms	8 months	cooked nuggets	3-4 months
Corn on the Cob	8-10 months	pre-stuffed chicken breasts	don't freeze
Herbs	6 months	cooked poultry dishes	4-6 months
Vegetable Purees	6-12 months	fresh chicken in marinade	2-3 months
Prepared Vegetable Dishes	3 months		
		Fish:	
Miscellaneous:		fresh pieces	6-12 months
Pasta, cooked	3-4 months	cooked pieces	2-3 months
Pasta, mixed into dishes	3-4 months	cooked fish dishes	2-3 months
Rice, cooked	3-4 months	fish in marinade	2-3 months
Rice, mixed into dishes	3-4 months		
		Miscellaneous:	
		vegetable or meat soups/stews	2-3 months
		ground veal and lamb	3-4 months
		gravy and meat broths	2-3 months
		cooked meat pies	3-4 months
		cooked meatloaf	1-3 months

For more extensive information on freezing, call the USDA Meat and Poultry Hotline. You can also request free information on safe food handling and power outage problems.
1-800-535-4555

BLANCHING CHART FOR VEGETABLES

Always choose good, quality, fresh vegetables. Clean and trim off inedible parts. Cut to desired uniformly sized pieces.

MICROWAVE BLANCHING
✓ Choose a round microwaveable bowl or container.
✓ Place 1/4 C. of water in the container.
✓ Into the container, place no more than 4 C. of leafy vegetables (like spinach) or 2 C. of other vegetables.
✓ Cover the container with microwaveable plastic wrap.
✓ Make sure that if you have a turntable, it can move freely.
✓ Microwave according to the chart below on highest power setting.
✓ After blanching, spread vegetables out in a single layer on a tray or baking sheet and cool 5 minutes. They are now suitable for freezing by themselves, or in a freezer recipe.

STOVE TOP STEAMING
✓ Prepare vegetable as above.
✓ Use a pan that a wire mesh basket or steamer basket will fit into (at least 8 qt. size).
✓ Bring 1 inch of water to a rolling boil in the pan.
✓ Place no more than 1 pound of vegetables in the basket and place over the steaming water.
✓ Time according to the chart below.
✓ Remove the basket of vegetables from the pot and plunge into cold or ice water, or run cold water over them. This stops the cooking action.
✓ Drain well. The vegetables are now ready for freezing or using in a freezer recipe.

BOILING WATER BLANCHING
✓ Clean and prepare vegetables as above.
✓ In a large pot, bring at least 1 gallon of water for every pound of vegetables to a rolling boil.
✓ Plunge the vegetables in the water 1 pound at a time.
✓ When the water begins to boil again, start timing according to the chart below.
✓ At the end of the blanching time, remove vegetables from the water with a slotted spoon, steamer basket, or strainer with a handle.
✓ Cool hot vegetables as for range top steaming. The vegetables are now ready for use in the freezer.

BLANCHING CHART

VEGETABLE	MICRO-STEAM	RANGE TOP STEAM	BOILING WATER
beets	n/a	n/a	30-45min.
broccoli	5 min.	3-5 min.	2-4 min.
brussels sprouts	4 min.	6 min.	4 min.
cabbage wedges	3 min.	4 min.	3 min.
carrots	2-5 min.	4-5 min.	2-5 min.
cauliflower	5 min.	5 min.	3 min.
celery	3 min.	4 min.	3 min.
corn on the cob	n/a	n/a	6-8 min.
corn cut from cob	4 min.	6 min.	4 min.
green beans	3 min.	4 min.	3 min.
peas, all types	4 min.	6 min.	4 min.
potatoes cubed/sliced/shredded	10 min.	12 min.	10 min.
spinach/other greens	n/a	3 min.	2 min.
sweet potatoes	Any method will work. Cook until soft.		
zucchini, cubed	2-3 min.	2-3 min.	2-3 min.

NO BLANCHING NEEDED FOR: mushrooms, onions, peppers, tomatoes, shredded zucchini
Note: If you live at a high altitude, add 30 seconds to the blanching time for every 1000 feet above sea level.

BASIC COOKING TERMS AND DEFINITIONS

One of the goals of this manual is for it to be so simple that only the most basic cooking skills are needed. Remember that only one of us claims to be a cook. If you are unfamiliar with any of the cooking terms used in this manual, you should be able to find their meanings written below:

Baste: Refers to spooning or brushing juices, pan drippings, stock, broth, butter, oil or marinade over meats, poultry or fish. You can use a brush, bulb syringe, bulb baster, or spoon for this job.

Beat: This means to mix rapidly to make a mixture smooth and light. In beating, air is incorporated into the mixture. Beating by hand should be done with a whisk, a fork, or a wooden spoon. Use your wrist in a quick up and down circular motion. An electric mixer is one of the greatest beating tools! Use a round bowl for beating, not a square or rectangular container. You will not get the corners mixed adequately.

Blanch: This means to boil rapidly in a good quantity of water. It destroys harmful enzymes in vegetables, helps to make peeling tomatoes or fruits easier, sets the color, and seals in juices and vitamins. See the blanching chart on page 131 for more complete instructions.

Blend: This means to mix two or more ingredients together so thoroughly that they become one product. This is most completely done with an electric blender or mixer. Blending by hand takes a long time!

Boil: This means to heat a liquid until bubbles constantly come to the surface. A slow boil means the bubbles lazily come to the surface. In a hard boil, the bubbles are large and rapidly break the surface.

Broil: Broiling is a cooking method using intense heat on one side. Broiling can be done in the stove, or on a grill. It is usually a quick cooking method that needs to be watched carefully to prevent burning.

Brown: The purpose of browning is to quickly sear the meat, sealing in juices and giving color to the food. Medium to high heat is usually used. Sometimes the heat is lowered to complete the cooking.

Broth: This is a liquid containing the flavors and aroma of chicken, beef, fish, or vegetables. The meat or vegetables are simmered in water, then the solids are strained out, leaving broth. Broth may be made from purchased granules or cubes that have been dissolved in water. Condensed broth is also available.

Chop: Chopping is cutting a solid object into pieces with a sharp knife. To chop efficiently, hold the blade of a large knife at both ends, bringing it up and down firmly over the food to be chopped.

Cream: This means to beat two or more ingredients together until smooth and creamy.

Cut in: Work butter, shortening, margarine, or lard into a flour mixture until it looks like coarse crumbs that are even in shape and texture.

De-grease: Removing grease or fat from a broth, soup, or sauce is called de-greasing. You can skim the fat off the top with a spoon or skimmer, or chill the liquid until the fat rises to the surface and hardens. The hard fat can be removed with a slotted spatula and discarded.

Dice: This is similar to chopping, but it usually results in fairly small pieces.

Dredge: This usually means to drag a solid food like meat, fruit, or vegetables through other dry ingredients like sugar or flour. This presses the dry ingredients into the food.

Drippings: These are the juices, fats, and browned bits of food left in a pan after cooking. The drippings are good for making sauces and gravies.

Fold: Folding is done when a substance that has a lot of air in it, like whipped cream or beaten egg whites, is mixed into a heavier ingredient, like a batter. A rubber spatula or large spoon can be used to carefully lift and mix in the airy ingredient.

Grate: This usually means to rub a solid food, like vegetables or cheese against a grater. A grater has sharp blades that cut the solid food into smaller pieces.

Lukewarm: This is a temperature that is neither cool nor warm, about body temperature.

Marinate: This means to cover food in a seasoned liquid that contains some form of acid, like fruit juice, wine, or vinegar. This is done to tenderize and flavor a food.

Mince: This means to chop very, very fine.

Pinch: As a measurement, it is a very small amount. It is the amount you can hold between your thumb and index finger.

Puree: This means to mash something until it is a uniformly smooth product. This is done with a blender, food processor, or food mill.

Reduce: Boil or simmer a liquid to reduce its volume and intensify its flavor.

Sauté: This is a slower form of frying, requiring lower heat and less fat.

Simmer: Simmering is a *very* slow boil. The bubbles should barely break the surface of the liquid.

Steam: This means to cook or heat food over boiling water, with the food not touching the water. This is a very healthy way to cook. Usually a steamer basket is used inside a pan that contains the boiling water and a lid is usually placed over the food to hold in the heat.

Stock: This is an intensely flavored broth. The liquid is simmered until much of it evaporates, leaving a stronger flavored product.

Whisk: This means to beat with a whisk or whip until the food is well mixed.

FREEZER SELECTION AND MAINTENANCE

Whether you are considering purchasing a brand-new freezer, or looking for a reliable used model, there are a few important things to consider. Plan to purchase your appliance from a dealer who services what he sells. Look for a well-known brand so that parts are not hard to find for repairs. If your freezer is new, fill out the warranty card and send it in to the manufacturer right away.

Construction
A freezer cabinet should be made of a wrap-around, one-piece structure. The compressor should be hermetically sealed so that it requires no maintenance from you. It should have leveling feet on the cabinet. The controls should be positioned so that you can reach them easily, but toddlers can't. Freezer door seals are usually magnetic. Make sure that the seal is tight on all edges. If you close a piece of paper in the door it should be held tightly.

"Frost-Free" vs. "Frost-Full"
Defrosting is a burdensome chore for most homeowners. Frost-free models eliminate the problem by utilizing small heaters that melt the ice periodically. Because of the drying action and heat, it is especially important to properly package food headed for a frost-free appliance. Frost-free models cost around 50% more to operate than standard freezers. Because it costs more to operate and to purchase a frost-free model, you will have to determine if the cost is worth it. Most people only have to defrost a freezer once or twice a year. Look for the Federal Trade Commission (FTC) label on the appliance. The label will tell you how many kilowatt-hours the appliance will use. The smaller the number listed, the less energy is used. You should never run a frost-free freezer in a place where the temperature goes below 60°F. The compressor will not be turned on enough to keep the food from thawing.

Capacity
Check the capacity of the freezer and buy the size that is most suited to your eating patterns. A nearly full freezer runs much more efficiently than a half full one. If you purchase a freezer that is too large for your use, it may have a lot of air space that you have to cool. The freezer has to work harder to keep air cool than food, so frozen air takes more energy than frozen food!

Upright Freezers
Uprights range in size from 12 to 30 cu ft. A sliding basket or drawer is very handy for bulky items. Some come with ice makers, but they are usually optional, and they do take up room. A benefit of upright freezers is that they take up less floor space than a chest freezer of the same capacity. Also, the food is easily stacked and distributed on the shelves, and it is easier to find what you need without digging. This is a great benefit for the shorter folks among us! The temperature in the door storage spaces will be a bit warmer than the temperature in the back.

Chest Freezers
The sizes for these models run from 5 to 28 cu. ft. They generally cost less to buy than upright models. You also have more useable space in a chest freezer, because you can pack it clear to the top if you like. Upright freezers have wasted room at the top of each shelf full of food. Chest freezers are also more cost efficient to operate. The frozen food is packed more tightly together, so it holds the chill in. Also, since heat rises, opening the lid of a chest freezer allows less cold air to escape than opening the door of an upright freezer. In a chest freezer, the top center section will generally be a little warmer than the rest of the freezer.

Tara's upright freezer with 90 family-sized entrees plus miscellaneous food items.

FREEZER SELECTION AND MAINTENANCE

Installment

Most people do not have the luxury of a large freezer in or near the kitchen. The room it takes up is a big consideration for where to place a freezer. Also, you want to make sure you don't have it in a spot that is too warm or too cold. If your freezer is in the kitchen, it will have to work harder because of the surrounding temperature. Any spot that is relatively cool, out of direct sunlight, dry, and well ventilated is a suitable one for a freezer. The freezer will actually run better if it is in a room that remains above 40°F. Think about where you will plug it in. A freezer should be plugged into its own, grounded outlet. A freezer should also have its own circuit so that an overload from another appliance does not shut it off. The outlet should be in a position that it is as protected as possible. No one (pets included) should be able to become tangled in the cord. An unseen pulled plug spells disaster for your frozen foods! You should not push a freezer tightly up against a wall, or into a corner. A freezer needs room to dispel heat into the air. It is a very good idea to decide *where* the freezer will go, before you decide on a size or type. It is a good idea to set the leveling feet so that it tips back slightly. This will cause the door to swing shut automatically.

Temperature Settings

0°F is a temperature that will keep the foods you store well protected. Even though water freezes at 32°F, destructive enzymes are not kept from harming your foods at that temperature. The lower the temperature, the longer the food will store well. A temperature of -5°F will keep quality even longer, but be aware that your electric bill will rise as the temperature lowers!

If you will be away from home for more than a couple of days, have a neighbor or friend check up on your freezer to make sure it is still running. Tara left on her honeymoon only to return to a defrosted chest freezer and soggy remains of her wedding cake!

Defrosting

Follow the manufacturer's instructions (if you have them) for defrosting. If your freezer is running well and the seal is in good shape, you should not have to defrost more than once or twice a year. You should defrost before the ice is 1/2" thick on the interior walls. This job will take anywhere from 2 to 3 hours, so allow plenty of time.

Here is a method that will work in the absence of the original manufacturer's instructions.
1. Plan to defrost your freezer at a time when it is fairly empty already.
2. For an extra safety precaution, wear rubber-soled shoes to keep you from sliding across the floor or from getting an electrical shock.
3. Remove the frozen food and place it in coolers, or wrap the food containers in several sheets of newsprint and pack it tightly into cardboard boxes or crates.
4. You need to shut off the power to the freezer, or unplug the appliance.
5. If you are working on a chest freezer, be sure to prop the lid open so that it can't come crashing down.
6. Place some old towels on the floor in front of the freezer and a rolled up towel on the bottom of an upright freezer next to the rubber door seal. This will keep water from pouring out the bottom.
7. Find a pot that will fit inside your freezer. Fill it with hot water and bring it to a boil on the stove. If the spot you will set the pot on is not covered with ice, use a thick potholder to insulate the surface. Carefully place the pot of boiling water in the freezer. The steam will help to melt the ice more quickly. You can move the pot of water around in the freezer compartment to help break up the ice. When the pot stops steaming, bring the water to a boil again and repeat the process.
8. After the steam from the boiling water has had a chance to do its work, try to pry the ice off the ceiling and sides with your hands.
9. If the ice is still to thick to break apart, use a rag dipped in very hot water to drench and melt the ice. You can use a bulb baster too. Draw boiling hot water into it, then squirt it over the ice. Just be very careful not to burn yourself. Repeat the hot water drenching until you are down to the bare surface.
10. If your freezer has a drip tray underneath it, empty it every once in a while to keep it from overflowing. If you need to, sop up the melted ice with a rag or sponge and squeeze the water into a bucket or tub.
11. Do not use an ice pick, screwdriver, hammer, or knife to break apart the ice. Besides the danger to yourself, you will probably damage the inside of your freezer! You might just mark up the inside, or you might even break right through a coolant line, which will release toxic fumes into the air and kill your freezer.
12. Dry out the compartment with a clean dry towel.

FREEZER SELECTION AND MAINTENANCE

Exterior Cleaning
When you are finished defrosting a freezer, it is a great time to clean and deodorize it also. If you can, drag the whole appliance away from the wall. Vacuum up the dirt and mop up the remaining grime. Remove the grate in the back that covers the compressor and fan. This is usually at the very top, or very bottom of the appliance. Use a vacuum cleaner with a nozzle attachment to remove the accumulated dust around the compressor and fan. Replace the cover. Use an all-purpose cleaner to safely clean the outside of the freezer. Vacuum the dust off the condenser coils. When you are done and everything is clean and dry, turn the power to the freezer back on or plug it back into its outlet. Turn the freezer back on and make sure the temperature control is set where you want it to be. Place the food back into the freezer.

Interior Cleaning
For food residues, use a paste made of baking soda and water. Use it like a scouring powder to scrub the food off. Rinse the baking soda mixture off with clean warm water and a sponge or a rag. A baking soda and water solution is also a good rinse for the entire freezer. Besides the cleaning it will get, the baking soda also helps to remove odors.

Stubborn Odors
If there are stubborn odors in the freezer that the baking soda did not remove, try these options one at a time so that there will not be any chemical reactions between them. Rinse out the freezer with clear water if needed and wipe it dry before trying another method.

1. Vinegar and water solution - mix one cup of vinegar with one gallon of water.
2. Household chlorine bleach - mix a half cup of bleach with one gallon of water.
3. Leave crumpled up black and white newsprint in the freezer with the door shut.
4. Place charcoal briquettes in a tub or pan and leave them in the freezer with the door shut.
5. Make a mild solution of dish washing liquid and water. Wash with the mixture, then rinse with clean water.

Sometimes the odor is impossible to remove. Food that has been in the freezer too long, food that has been improperly packaged, or food that has spoiled in a power outage can cause lasting odors. If smelly moisture is absorbed by the freezer insulation, it may have strong permanent odors. You can either have the insulation replaced by an appliance repairman, or live with the problem. If you choose to put up with the odor, try to double wrap all of the foods in the freezer. When you take the food from the freezer, discard the outer wrapper. Hopefully *it* will contain the odor, not the inner wrap and food beneath it.

The main disadvantage of chest freezers is that you practically have to fall in to choose your dinner!

MISCELLANEOUS FREEZING QUESTIONS

How Do I Thaw My Frozen Foods?

Do you know how to safely thaw your frozen dinner entrees, side dishes and other frozen items? Here are some guidelines:

✓ Do not thaw meat or poultry at room temperature on the counter. Bacteria can multiply rapidly.
✓ The safest way to thaw meat or poultry is to defrost it in the refrigerator. Place the package in the refrigerator immediately after removing it from the freezer. If there is a possibility of leaking packages, place them in a metal pan or tray to catch the moisture.
✓ Foods that have been thawed in the refrigerator can be safely refrozen. You may still lose a little quality in flavor or texture.
✓ For faster thawing, put the package in a water-tight plastic bag submerged in cold water. Change the water every 30 minutes. The cold water temperature slows bacteria growth that may occur on the outer thawed portions while the inner areas are still thawing.
✓ The microwave oven can be used for quick, safe defrosting. Microwave ovens vary, so follow the manufacturer's suggestions for your specific model. Food defrosted in the microwave oven should be cooked immediately after thawing.

Can I Put My Frozen Entrees Directly In The Oven Or Microwave Oven?

When cooking frozen meat or poultry that has not been defrosted, you will need to cook it about 1½ times the length of time required for the same recipe when thawed. Here is another baking guide for frozen casseroles: A one-quart casserole dish will take about 1¼ hours, a 2-quart casserole takes about 1½ or 2 hours, and a 3-quart casserole will take around 2 to 2½ hours.

If you place a frozen glass, clay, or ceramic dish in a hot oven, it may shatter. Foods frozen in these containers should be at least partially thawed before placing in a hot oven. You can often place a frozen dish in an *unheated* oven and then turn the oven on to the regular temperature - do *NOT* use the preheat level! If you wish to cook frozen foods in a microwave oven, be sure the dishes they are frozen in are microwave safe! It will take 1/3 to 1/2 additional cooking time to bring them up to 150 to 160°F for serving. If there is a temperature probe available to you, be sure to use it. Do not force a temperature probe into frozen food. You may damage the probe and get an inaccurate reading. If possible, stir your food several times during the microwave reheating process. If your recipe is a layered dish like lasagna, and you cannot stir it, be sure to rotate the dish a quarter turn several times during the cooking process. When the cooking is completed, cover the dish with a lid or plastic wrap and observe the normal standing time recommended for the food. This will ensure even and complete cooking. If your casseroles seem a little dry during this long cooking time, you can pour 1/4 to 1/2 cup of milk, broth, or water over a six-serving recipe.

Does Freezing Kill Germs?

Freezing *does not* reliably kill all germs that may be present in foods. Freezing *will* prevent germs from multiplying and growing if the food is kept at a temperature of 0°F or less. When the food is thawed, any surviving bacteria can begin to grow and multiply again. It is important that you eat thawed entrees within two or three days and they should be stored in the refrigerator.

What Is Freezer Burn?

Freezer burn is dehydration that occurs on the surface of food if it is improperly packaged, or if the packaging becomes torn, cracked, or a seal pops open. Freezer burned food is safe to eat, but the "burned" portion will suffer in flavor, texture, and appearance. Sometimes the freezer burned portion can be cut away and discarded. The remaining food may be just fine. To prevent freezer burn, the freezer packaging must be vapor and moisture proof, and free of excess air.

Why Are Ice Crystals On My Food?

Harmless ice crystals can form on frozen food for a number of different reasons. If excess water is not drained from blanched vegetables, they may have an ice accumulation. If the freezer is stocked with too great a quantity of warm or room temperature foods, the freezing time may be slow and that can cause crystals to appear. If the temperature in the freezer fluctuates greatly because of a power outage ice crystals may occur. Don't remove them. Let this moisture melt back into the food.

What If I Don't Have The Pan Size That Is Specified In The Recipe?

If the recipe calls for a 4-cup baking dish, use a 9" pie pan, an 8" round cake pan, or a 7-1/2 x 4" loaf pan. If the recipe calls for a 6-cup baking dish, use a 10" pie pan, a 9" round cake pan, or an 8½ x 3½" loaf pan. If the recipe calls for an 8-cup baking dish, you can use an 8 x 8 x 2" square cake pan, a 9" square cake pan, or a 9 x 5" loaf pan. When in doubt, measure water into a dish to see how much it will hold!

POWER FAILURE!

Without power, a full upright or chest freezer will keep everything frozen for about 2 days. A half full freezer will keep food frozen 1 day. If the power will be coming back on fairly soon, you can make the food last longer by keeping the door shut as much as possible and covering the unit with blankets and quilts. Make sure that you do not block the air vent. Use pins to keep the coverings away from the vent.
If the power will be off for an extended period, take the food to friends' freezers, locate a commercial freezer, or use dry ice.
Without power, a refrigerator will keep food cool for 4-6 hours depending on the kitchen temperature. A full, well-functioning freezer unit above a refrigerator should keep food frozen for 2 days. A half full one will keep food frozen for about 1 day. If you have access to it, block ice can keep food on the refrigerator shelves cooler.

Locate the closest place to get dry ice *before* it becomes a necessity. Use up to 25 pounds of dry ice in a 10 cubic foot freezer. Place 50 pounds of dry ice in a 20 cubic foot freezer. Only use dry ice if the freezer is in a well ventilated spot. Dry ice is solid carbon dioxide. When it melts it becomes carbon dioxide gas that can cause suffocation in a small, enclosed room. If there is not enough ventilation, some signs of a carbon dioxide problem might be rapid, shallow breathing, a headache, or feeling disoriented. If the problem is allowed to progress, it might result in unconsciousness, and eventually death! Please be careful! You can't touch dry ice so be sure to wear heavy gloves. Wrap the dry ice in newsprint and place it on a board or several thicknesses of cardboard or a piece of board. Set the board on the food packages. Close the door of the freezer and do not open it again unless absolutely needed. If your freezer is half full, the dry ice should keep the temperature below freezing for 2-3 days. If the freezer is full, it should stay frozen for 3-4 days. Follow the handling instructions carefully!
The length of time that your food stays frozen also depends on what type of food is in your freezer. Meats stay frozen longer than fruits, vegetables and breads.

Re-freezing Foods
As a general rule, if the power has been off for quite a while, and then comes back on, food still containing ice crystals or that feel refrigerator-cold can be refrozen. Do not be surprised if a little quality is lost in re-freezing. Discard any thawed food that has risen to room temperature and remained so two hours or more. Immediately throw out anything with a strange color or odor. Before you begin to re-freeze food, be sure to turn the freezer to its coldest temperature. Mark the foods as "re-frozen". Space the food out on the shelves so that air can flow freely around the packages. When all the foods are solidly re-frozen, return the temperature setting to its normal position.

Meats - To re-freeze meats, re-package them in freezer bags, or tightly sealed rigid freezer containers. Do not refreeze ground meats that have thawed. Only re-freeze ground meat packages that are still solidly frozen. Icy cold packages of thawed meat can be cooked thoroughly, then re-packaged for the freezer.

Cured Meats - Ham, bacon, hard salami, and pepperoni can be re-frozen if they are still cold to the touch.

Poultry – Re-package icy poultry in moisture-vapor proof packaging before re-freezing. Leave the original wrapping on it, but place it inside a freezer bag or rigid freezer container. Discard any poultry that has come to room temperature. If poultry juices have dripped onto other foods, treat them like thawed poultry - throw them out! If the poultry is still cold, cook and eat it right away, or cook it and freeze immediately.

Fish - Do not re-freeze fish unless it is still solidly frozen. If the fish is thawed, but very cold to the touch, cook it and consume immediately. Throw out any fish that has come to room temperature.

Fruits - Use thawed fruits to make jams, jellies, preserves, or cooked pie fillings.

Vegetables - You can re-freeze vegetables that still have ice crystals in them. If the vegetables are thawed but still in good condition, you can cook and eat them.

Miscellaneous - Completely thawed baked goods, dinner entrees, juices and cheese should not be re-frozen. If they are still cold, they should be refrigerated and eaten as soon as possible. Do not eat dinner entrees that have thawed to room temperature.

A MONTH OF BREAKFAST AND LUNCH IDEAS!

Do you struggle with serving the same old stuff every day for breakfast and lunch? Tired of toast and juice, or peanut butter and jelly? Why not schedule a rotation for these two meal chores. Maybe you can pick out your 14 favorite breakfasts and lunches and place them on the calendar. This will eliminate the decision-making in the early hours of the day and aid you in shopping. You can make sure you have what you need on-hand for these meals. This is another great use for the *Meal Planning Calendar* in your worksheet section. Post it on your refrigerator, or some other safe place and refer to it in the morning to know what you will have to do to prepare in advance for these meals.

Breakfast Ideas
Oatmeal with raisins
Pancakes with syrup ✳ ◆
French toast with fruit toppings ✳
Breakfast pizza (sausage and ham are good) ✳
Hard boiled eggs and toast
Bacon and blueberry muffins ✳ ◆
Fried eggs and biscuits ✳ ◆
Breakfast burritos ✳
English muffins and scrambled eggs
Bacon and toast
Biscuits ✳ ◆ and bacon
Breakfast egg casserole ✳
Hashbrowns and eggs
Cold cereal
Bread pudding ✳
Cream of wheat with fruit
Breakfast McBiscuits ✳ ◆
Fruit cobbler ✳ ◆
Cheese toast and fruit juice
Grilled peanut butter and jelly sandwiches
Granola cereal ✳ ◆ with milk and fruit
Scrambled egg, cooked with sliced link sausages
Granola bars ✳ ◆
Waffles ✳ ◆ and syrup
Potato pancakes ✳ and applesauce
Scrambled eggs with diced ham
Cinnamon rolls ✳
Scrambled eggs with cheese
Drop biscuits with cheese ✳ ◆
Sausage in a blanket (rolled in a pancake) ✳ ◆
Biscuits ✳ ◆ with sausage gravy
Bagels ✳ and bacon
Toasted banana bread ✳
Cornbread ✳ with warm syrup and butter
Apple squares ✳ ◆

Lunch Ideas
Spaghetti with marinara sauce ✳
Grilled cheese sandwiches
Chicken noodle soup ✳ and half a ham sandwich
Vegetable soup ✳ and breadsticks ✳
Macaroni and cheese ✳ ◆
Tuna salad sandwiches
Pasta/veggie salad
Peanut butter and jelly sandwiches on whole wheat
Taco salad ✳ ◆ (try using our Taco Rice recipe)
Burritos ✳
Baked potatoes with toppings
Cheese filled shells ✳ ◆
Baked ziti ✳
Cheeseburger quiche ✳ ◆
Sloppy joes ✳ (meat portion can be frozen)
Chicken nuggets ✳ ◆ and tater tots ✳
Breaded fish fillets ✳ ◆ and oven fries
Baked cheese sticks ✳ ◆ and tossed green salad
Tacos ✳ (meat and cheese can be frozen)
Cheeseburgers ✳ (meat only) and homefries ✳
Ham quiche ✳
Seafood/pasta salad
Veggie or cheese pizza ✳
Nachos ✳ (meat and cheese are freezeable)
Hot dogs ✳ and French fries ✳
Grilled ham and cheese sandwiches
Bbq pork ✳ ◆ sandwiches
Bean and bacon soup ✳
Chicken salad in pita bread
Beef vegetable soup ✳ and corn muffins ✳
French bread pizza ✳
Bread sticks ✳ with marinara sauce ✳, and cole slaw
Stir fry veggies over rice ✳ (cooked rice is freezeable)
Chef salad
Hot buttered noodles and frozen fruit salad ✳ ◆

Feel free to substitute lunch items for breakfast items. There is no law stating that waffles are only for breakfast or grilled cheese sandwiches are only for lunch! Use your creativity to come up with your own list of favorites. The items that are marked with ✳ can be frozen. The ones marked with ◆ are recipes that can be found in this manual.

Once a week or so, you can look over your lunch and breakfast choices and make a shopping list that includes any items you will need.

FOOD COOPERATIVE INFORMATION

There are some great reasons to belong to a food buying club. A few that we've found are:

✓ We have access to hundreds of healthy foods. Supermarkets who carry healthy foods rarely offer very many choices or low prices. Food cooperatives have both!
✓ We can purchase large quantities for bulk rates. The food will be cheaper in most cases because many households are buying together and guaranteeing a minimum dollar amount purchase. Food Cooperative warehouses sell and deliver foods to local food buying clubs that individuals become members of.
✓ We make fewer trips to specialty markets or health food stores for unusual or ethnic food items.

How to find a food cooperative in your area?
Contact the National Cooperative Business Association by email at ncba@ncba.org or visit their web page to view a list of several cooperative warehouses and the different areas they serve. http://www.cooperative.org/fwhole.cfm. All 50 states are served by one warehouse or another. Here is a list of the ones we are familiar with:

COOPERATIVE WAREHOUSE	LOCATION	TELEPHONE #	AREAS OF SERVICE
Blooming Prairie Natural Foods	Minneapolis, MN	612.378.9774	Serving IA, IL, KS, MI, MN, MO, NE, ND, SD, WI
Blooming Prairie Warehouse, Inc	Iowa City, IA	319.337.6448	Serving east ND, SD, northern WI, northern MI
E&S Sales	1235 N. St. Rd. 5 Shipshewana, IN 46565	Mail Order Only	Entire United States
Federation of Ohio River Cooperatives (FORC)	Columbus, OH	614.861.2446	Serving IN, KY, MD, MI, NC, OH, PA, SC, VA, WV
Frontier Cooperative Herbs	Norway, IA	319.227.7991	Entire United States
Hudson Valley Federation of Food Cooperatives	Poughkeepsie, NY	914.473.5400	CT, NJ, NY, PA
Mountain People's Northwest	Auburn, WA	800.336.8872	Serving AK, AZ, CA, CO, HA, ID, MT, NV, NM, OR, UT, WY
Mountains People's Warehouse	Auburn, CA	530.889.9531	Most southwestern states
North Farm Co-op Warehouse	Madison, WI	800.236.5880	Serving IL, IN, MI, MN, WI; parts of MO, OH, ND, SD, WY, MT, IA
Northeast Cooperatives, Inc.	Battleboro, VT	800.334.9939	Serving, CT, MA, NH, NY, RI, VT
Ozark Co-op Warehouse	Fayetteville, AR	501.521.4920	AL, AR, FL, GA, KS, LA, MO, MS, OK, TN, TX
Rainbow Distributing	Chicago, IL	773.929.7629	Most midwestern states
Something Better Natural Foods	Battle Creek, MI	616.965.1199	Serving OH, TN, IN, NC, KY
Tucson Cooperative Warehouse	Tucson, AZ	602.884.9951	Serving AZ , southern CA, CO, NM, NV, TX, UT

Some of the food items we regularly purchase from cooperatives through our local food buying clubs are flour, pasta, dried beans, rice, seasonings and herbs, soy meat substitutes, cooking oils, tortillas, and flavoring extracts.

We're on the Web...

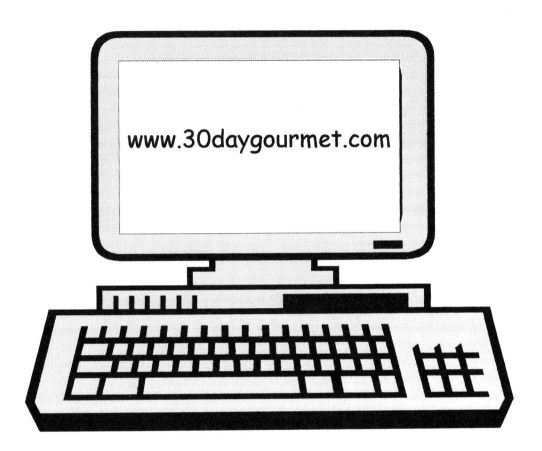

www.30daygourmet.com

- ◆ **More recipes**
    User name: recipes
    Password: macaroni
- ◆ **Message Boards**
- ◆ **Chat Room**
- ◆ **E-mail the Authors:**
    office@30daygourmet.com
- ◆ **Photo Album**
- ◆ **Speaking Schedule**

30 DAY GOURMET ORDER FORM
Send to: P.O. Box 272, Brownsburg, IN 46112
Fax to: 1-317-852-1946
Call toll-free: 1-800-9-MANUAL
Website: www.30daygourmet.com

The FREEZER COOKING MANUAL from 30 DAY GOURMET $14.95
Our comprehensive system for assembling and freezing 4-6 weeks' worth of tasty, nutritious entrees, side dishes and snacks in an easy-to-follow format. Includes:

- Time Saving Worksheets
- Step-By-Step Instructions
- 60+ Delicious Recipes
- Cooking Tips & Practical Money-Saving Advice
- 100+ Equivalents
- Master Mixes
- 20+ Easy Sauces & Marinades
- Indispensable Tally Sheet
- Nutritious Snacks
- 20 Photos

30 DAY GOURMET COOKING APRONS $20.00
- Style 1: "30 DAY GOURMET" logo
- Style 2: "Great Cooks Do It Once-A-Month" with 30 Day Gourmet logo

Color: Royal Blue with dark yellow print   *Adjustable Neck Strap*
Material: Durable poly/ cotton, washable   *Size: 30" X 36" (knee length)*

30 DAY GOURMET HOLIDAY COOKING BOOK $8.00
Our system for assembling and freezing your entire holiday meal. No more all night cooking. Make dinner when you have the time! Out traditional feasts serve 6 – 36 guests without the traditional hassle. Includes:
- Easy Step-By-Step Instructions
- 26 Delicious recipes to feed 6-36 guests
- Freezing and Cooking Tips
- Low-fat Alternatives

30 DAY GOURMET *LIVE* VIDEO $19.95
90 minute seminar/teaching video full of fun and great information. Nanci and Tara walk you step-by-step through 30 Day Gourmet plan. It covers:
- Choosing Recipes
- Assembling in Quantity
- Buddy System Benefits
- Shopping Smart
- Freezing for Great Results

30 DAY GOURMET CONSULTANT KIT $100.00
All you need to host a successful seminar about 30 Day Gourmet cooking. Includes:
- 2 Freezer Cooking Manuals
- "Great Cooks Do It Once A Month" Apron
- 90 Minute Seminar/Teaching Video
- Comprehensive Consultant Planner
- 5 Seminar Posters
- Folder Full of Supplies & Publicity Helps
- 2 Holiday Cooking Books
- "30 Day Gourmet Apron" (Personally Monogrammed)
- Book Display Easel
- 25 Recipe/Price Sheets
- 25 Postcard Invitations

PACKAGE DEALS:
Package Deal #1 – Two Manuals $27.90 (save $2.00)
Package Deal #2 – Manual & Holiday Book $20.00 (save $2.95)
Package Deal #3 - Manual, Holiday Book, & Apron $35.00 (save $7.95)

BULK ORDERS:
10+ Freezer Cooking Manuals at 50%   **$7.50 each**
10+ Holiday Cooking Books at 50%   **$4.00 each**
5+ Videos at 50%   **$10.00 each**
5+ Aprons at 40%   **$12.00 each**

over for order form

Please fill out completely and send or fax to us.

Date:

Customer Name:

Address:

City:	State:	Zip Code:

Telephone Number: Home (   ) _____ - _____

Work (_____) _____ - _____

E-mail address:

QTY	DESCRIPTION	PRICE	TOTAL
	Pkg. 1 – 2 Manuals (save $2.00)	$27.90	
	Pkg. 2 – Manual & Holiday Book (save $2.95)	$20.00	
	Pkg. 3 – Manual, Holiday Book, & Apron (save $7.95) Which apron? _____	$35.00	
	30 Day Gourmet Cooking Manual	$14.95	
	Each Additional Manual	$12.95	
	30 Day Gourmet Holiday Book	$8.00	
	Apron – "Great Cooks Do It Once A Month"	$20.00	
	Apron – "30 Day Gourmet"	$20.00	
	Video	$19.95	
	Consultant Kit	$100.00	

Priority Mail	2-3 days	Standard Mail	7-10 days		SUB TOTAL	
Purchase	Rate	Purchase	Rate		Priority Mail or	
Up to $23.95	$5.00	Up to $19.95	$3.00		Standard Mail	
$24.00-$35.95	$6.00	$20.00-$39.95	$4.00		5% Tax (IN only)	
$36.00-$47.95	$7.00	$40.00-$59.95	$5.00			
$48.00 & up	15%	$60.00 & up	10%		TOTAL	

Prices subject to change without notice.

Payment Method: ☐ Master Card   ☐Visa   ☐Discover   ☐AmEx
☐ Personal Check   ☐Money Order

Card Number: ☐☐☐☐–☐☐☐☐–☐☐☐☐–☐☐☐☐

Expiration Date: __ __ / __ __   Cardholder Signature: _____

How did you hear about 30 Day Gourmet? _____

Send to: P.O. Box 272, Brownsburg, IN 46112
Fax to: 1-317-852-1946
Call toll-free: 1-800-9-MANUAL
Website: www.30daygourmet.com

OFFICIALLY NOTED